VOCABULARY WORKBOOK FOR KIDS:

180 Word of the Day Vocabulary Activities

Noteworthy Vocabulary-Building for Upper Elementary

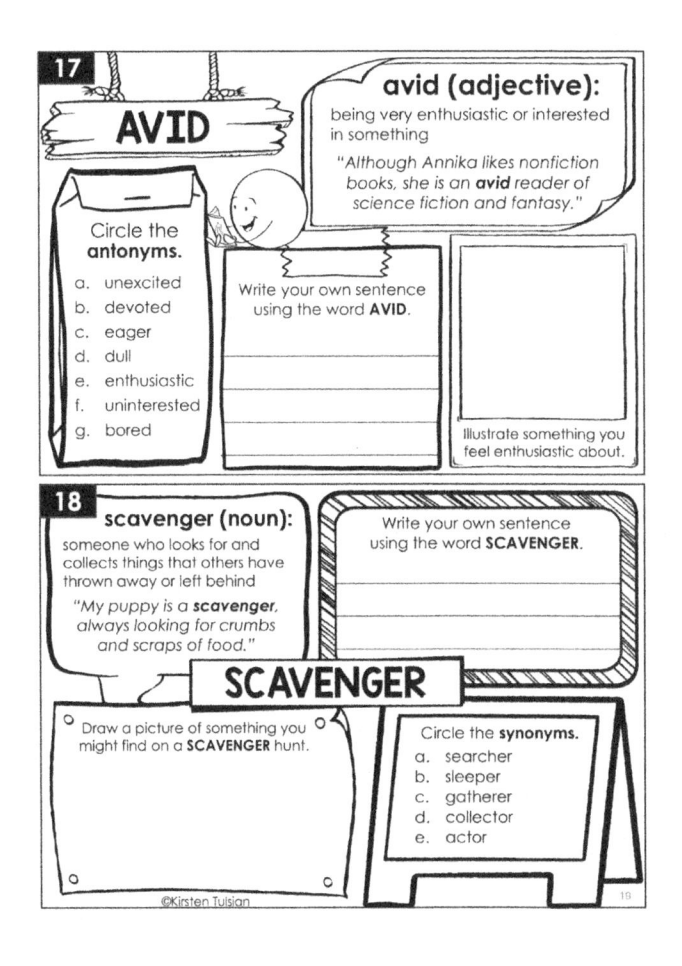

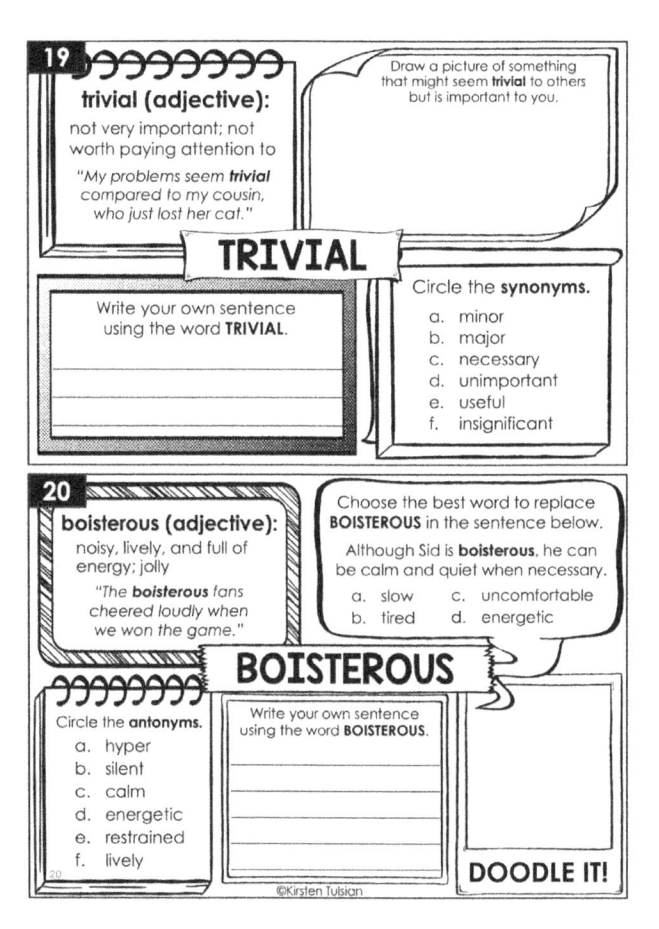

---

17 AVID

avid (adjective): being very enthusiastic or interested in something

"Although Annika likes nonfiction books, she is an **avid** reader of science fiction and fantasy."

Circle the **antonyms**.
a. unexcited
b. devoted
c. eager
d. dull
e. enthusiastic
f. uninterested
g. bored

Write your own sentence using the word AVID.

Illustrate something you feel enthusiastic about.

---

18 scavenger (noun): someone who looks for and collects things that others have thrown away or left behind

"My puppy is a **scavenger**, always looking for crumbs and scraps of food."

Write your own sentence using the word SCAVENGER.

SCAVENGER

Draw a picture of something you might find on a SCAVENGER hunt.

Circle the **synonyms**.
a. searcher
b. sleeper
c. gatherer
d. collector
e. actor

---

19 trivial (adjective): not very important; not worth paying attention to

"My problems seem **trivial** compared to my cousin, who just lost her cat."

Draw a picture of something that might seem **trivial** to others but is important to you.

TRIVIAL

Write your own sentence using the word TRIVIAL.

Circle the **synonyms**.
a. minor
b. major
c. necessary
d. unimportant
e. useful
f. insignificant

---

20 boisterous (adjective): noisy, lively, and full of energy; jolly

"The **boisterous** fans cheered loudly when we won the game."

Choose the best word to replace BOISTEROUS in the sentence below.

Although Sid is **boisterous**, he can be calm and quiet when necessary.
a. slow   c. uncomfortable
b. tired   d. energetic

BOISTEROUS

Circle the **antonyms**.
a. hyper
b. silent
c. calm
d. energetic
e. restrained
f. lively

Write your own sentence using the word BOISTEROUS.

DOODLE IT!

©Kirsten Tulsian. All rights reserved.

© Kirsten Tulsian, Kirsten's Kaboodle, 2025-Present.
All Rights Reserved.

Images and cover art created by Sarah Pecorino Illustration. The purchase of this publication entitles the buyer to reproduce pages in this book for single classroom use ONLY. No other part of this publication may be reproduced in whole or in part, stored in a retrieval system, or distributed or transmitted in any form or by any means. This includes electronic, photocopying, recording, or other electronic or mechanical methods without prior permission from the publisher.

No part of this product may be used or reproduced for commercial use.

Contact the author:
Kirsten's Kaboodle
kirsten@kirstenskaboodle.com
PO Box 91193
Salt Lake City, UT 84109

THIS BOOK BELONGS TO:

TIPS FOR USE

Research indicates a strong correlation between vocabulary knowledge and reading comprehension. Vocabulary development is also crucial for language and speaking skills and overall academic success.

This workbook contains **180 vocabulary words**, their parts of speech, definitions, sample sentences, and related activities. If used each weekday, this workbook will take 36 weeks to complete, which covers a typical school year consisting of 180 days.

SYNONYMS AND ANTONYMS: It's important to note that there are very few "true" or "perfect" synonyms. Synonyms mean **the same or nearly the same thing** as a given word. Likewise, antonyms mean **the opposite or nearly the opposite** of a given word. Perfect synonyms and perfect antonyms rarely exist.

Children will need access to a dictionary (online dictionaries work well). The sections related to synonyms and antonyms may include unknown words. Dictionary access will help children complete those tasks. In addition to learning the new word of the day, they will also learn several new related words.

DOODLE IT: In the picture/doodle sections, please allow children to use their imaginations. There are no rules about incorporating the vocabulary words or ideas into their doodles. I recommend regular or colored pencils, as markers and pens may bleed through the page.

NOTE: Several vocabulary words have multiple meanings. For the purposes of this workbook, each entry focuses on **ONE** meaning (often the most relevant meaning for the intended age range). You can encourage your child(ren) to identify words with multiple meanings if you choose.

If you have any questions, please don't hesitate to contact me at kirsten@kirstenskaboodle.com. You can also find related PDF resources at kirstenskaboodle.com.

©Kirsten Tulsian

Vocabulary Word List:

1. queasy
2. significant
3. withdraw
4. wisdom
5. motive
6. outstanding
7. absurd
8. turbulent
9. stint
10. achievement
11. beneficial
12. profound
13. tranquil
14. ambitious
15. embark
16. encounter
17. avid
18. scavenger
19. trivial
20. boisterous
21. massive
22. grotesque
23. convince
24. continuous
25. decay
26. acknowledge
27. flustered
28. astound
29. venture
30. rejuvenate
31. investigate
32. maintain
33. aloof
34. precision
35. remorse
36. predict
37. bizarre
38. discreet
39. anguish
40. nurture
41. bland
42. obnoxious
43. rigorous
44. disgruntled
45. efficient
46. pedestrian
47. devour
48. debris
49. epic
50. exquisite

©Kirsten Tulsian

Vocabulary Word List:

51. potential
52. awkward
53. immense
54. beckon
55. suitable
56. peculiar
57. abrupt
58. examine
59. banter
60. subtle
61. duplicate
62. unbelievable
63. distraught
64. sturdy
65. detect
66. vibrant
67. triumph
68. fascinate
69. navigate
70. ordeal
71. perceptive
72. meander
73. recite
74. obvious
75. exclude
76. murky
77. enhance
78. scoff
79. perplexed
80. hazardous
81. lurk
82. noteworthy
83. vivid
84. bewilder
85. agile
86. solitary
87. retrieve
88. rubble
89. lure
90. visible
91. provoke
92. discard
93. reluctant
94. miniature
95. identical
96. illuminate
97. irate
98. wander
99. essential
100. destructive

Vocabulary Word List:

101. exaggerate
102. benefit
103. swelter
104. dollop
105. tidy
106. effective
107. fabulous
108. transform
109. tragic
110. enable
111. jagged
112. fortunate
113. expand
114. indulge
115. envy
116. tender
117. hazy
118. linger
119. blunder
120. perish
121. plead
122. avoid
123. hostile
124. fiasco
125. arid
126. wrangle
127. frantic
128. lethargic
129. swarm
130. acquire
131. abandon
132. anxious
133. empathy
134. feeble
135. strive
136. notify
137. unruly
138. prevent
139. sensitive
140. mimic
141. recycle
142. pursue
143. plentiful
144. prosper
145. haven
146. burden
147. dazzle
148. clarify
149. contribute
150. doze

Vocabulary Word List:

151. unique
152. arrogant
153. vast
154. consult
155. cope
156. brilliant
157. delicate
158. ponder
159. disturbance
160. erupt
161. drift
162. attempt
163. miraculous
164. ferocious
165. priority
166. agitate
167. confident
168. bamboozle
169. hoax
170. complex
171. scarce
172. magnificent
173. pending
174. atypical
175. vicious
176. declare
177. durable
178. rupture
179. equivalent
180. shenanigans

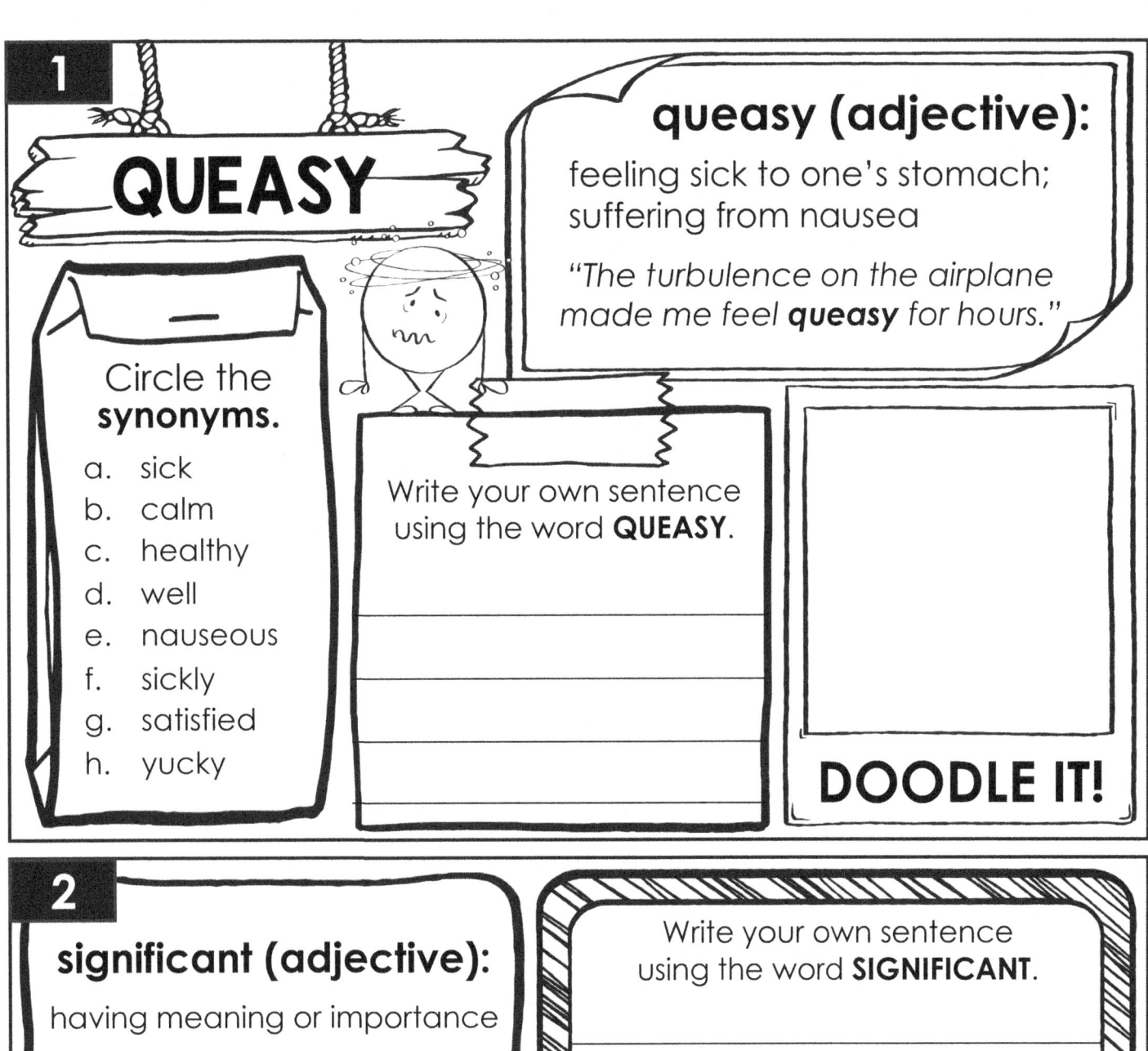

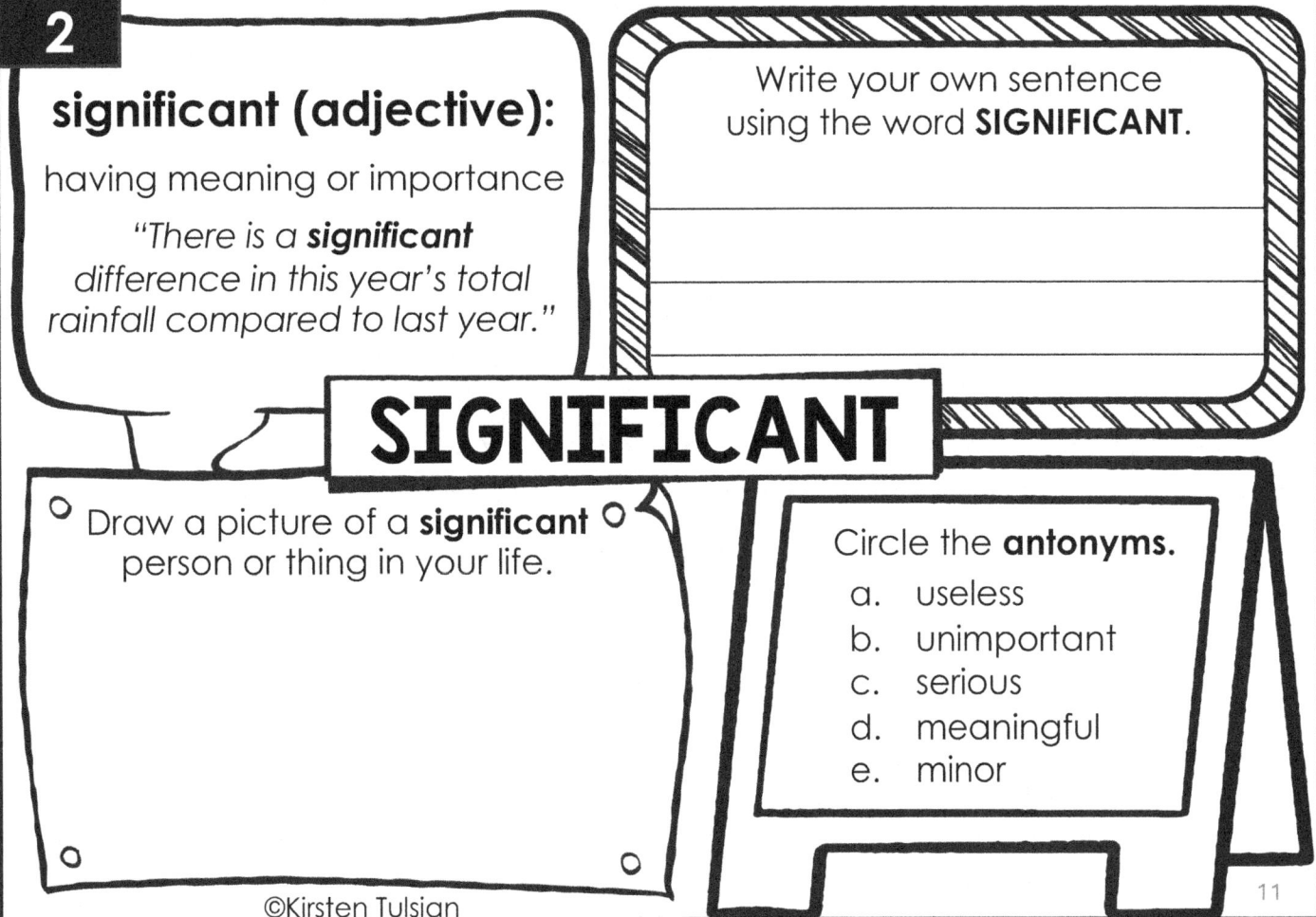

1

QUEASY

queasy (adjective): feeling sick to one's stomach; suffering from nausea

*"The turbulence on the airplane made me feel **queasy** for hours."*

Circle the **synonyms**.
a. sick
b. calm
c. healthy
d. well
e. nauseous
f. sickly
g. satisfied
h. yucky

Write your own sentence using the word **QUEASY**.

DOODLE IT!

2

significant (adjective): having meaning or importance

*"There is a **significant** difference in this year's total rainfall compared to last year."*

Write your own sentence using the word **SIGNIFICANT**.

SIGNIFICANT

Draw a picture of a **significant** person or thing in your life.

Circle the **antonyms**.
a. useless
b. unimportant
c. serious
d. meaningful
e. minor

©Kirsten Tulsian

3. WITHDRAW

withdraw (verb): to draw back, step aside, or back away

"I would like to **withdraw** my entry for the talent show."

Make a list of three things you might **withdraw** from in your life.

1.
2.
3.

Write your own sentence using the word **WITHDRAW**.

Circle the **synonyms.**
a. drop out
b. quit
c. begin
d. leave
e. continue
f. stay

4. WISDOM

wisdom (noun): good understanding and judgment

"Grandma's **wisdom** comes from decades of experience, living, and learning."

Choose the best word to replace **WISDOM** in the sentence below.

Uncle Ralph shares so many nuggets of **wisdom** from his 100-year life.

a. insight   c. confusion
b. boredom   d. anger

Circle the **antonyms.**
a. insight
b. experience
c. stupidity
d. ignorance
e. knowledge
f. intelligence

Write your own sentence using the word **WISDOM**.

DOODLE IT!

©Kirsten Tulsian

5

motive (noun): the reason why someone does something

*"Ellie's **motive** for running away was to avoid punishment for a bad grade."*

DOODLE IT!

MOTIVE

Write your own sentence using the word **MOTIVE**.

Choose the best word to replace **MOTIVE** in the sentence below.

Her **motive** for working two jobs is to pay the bills.

a. reason
b. excuse
c. journey
d. detour

6

outstanding (adjective): exceptionally good; incredible

*"The painting was an **outstanding** display of the artist's creativity and talent."*

Choose the best word to replace **OUTSTANDING** in the sentence below.

My little brother's talent show performance was **outstanding**!

a. marginal
b. good
c. fantastic
d. great

DOODLE IT!

OUTSTANDING

Write your own sentence using the word **OUTSTANDING**.

©Kirsten Tulsian

7

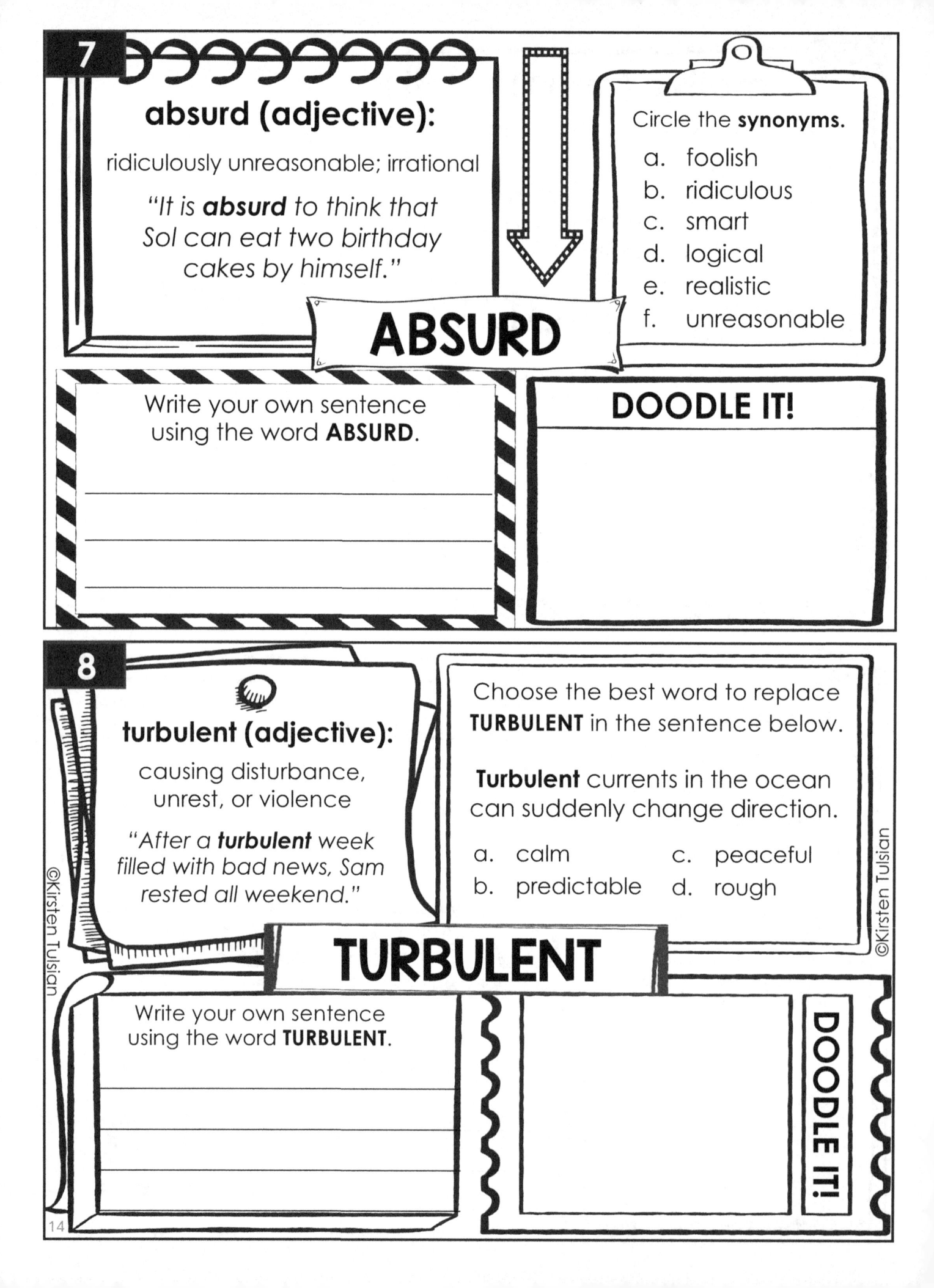

absurd (adjective):

ridiculously unreasonable; irrational

"It is **absurd** to think that Sol can eat two birthday cakes by himself."

ABSURD

Circle the **synonyms**.
a. foolish
b. ridiculous
c. smart
d. logical
e. realistic
f. unreasonable

Write your own sentence using the word **ABSURD**.

DOODLE IT!

8

turbulent (adjective):

causing disturbance, unrest, or violence

"After a **turbulent** week filled with bad news, Sam rested all weekend."

TURBULENT

Choose the best word to replace **TURBULENT** in the sentence below.

Turbulent currents in the ocean can suddenly change direction.

a. calm
b. predictable
c. peaceful
d. rough

Write your own sentence using the word **TURBULENT**.

DOODLE IT!

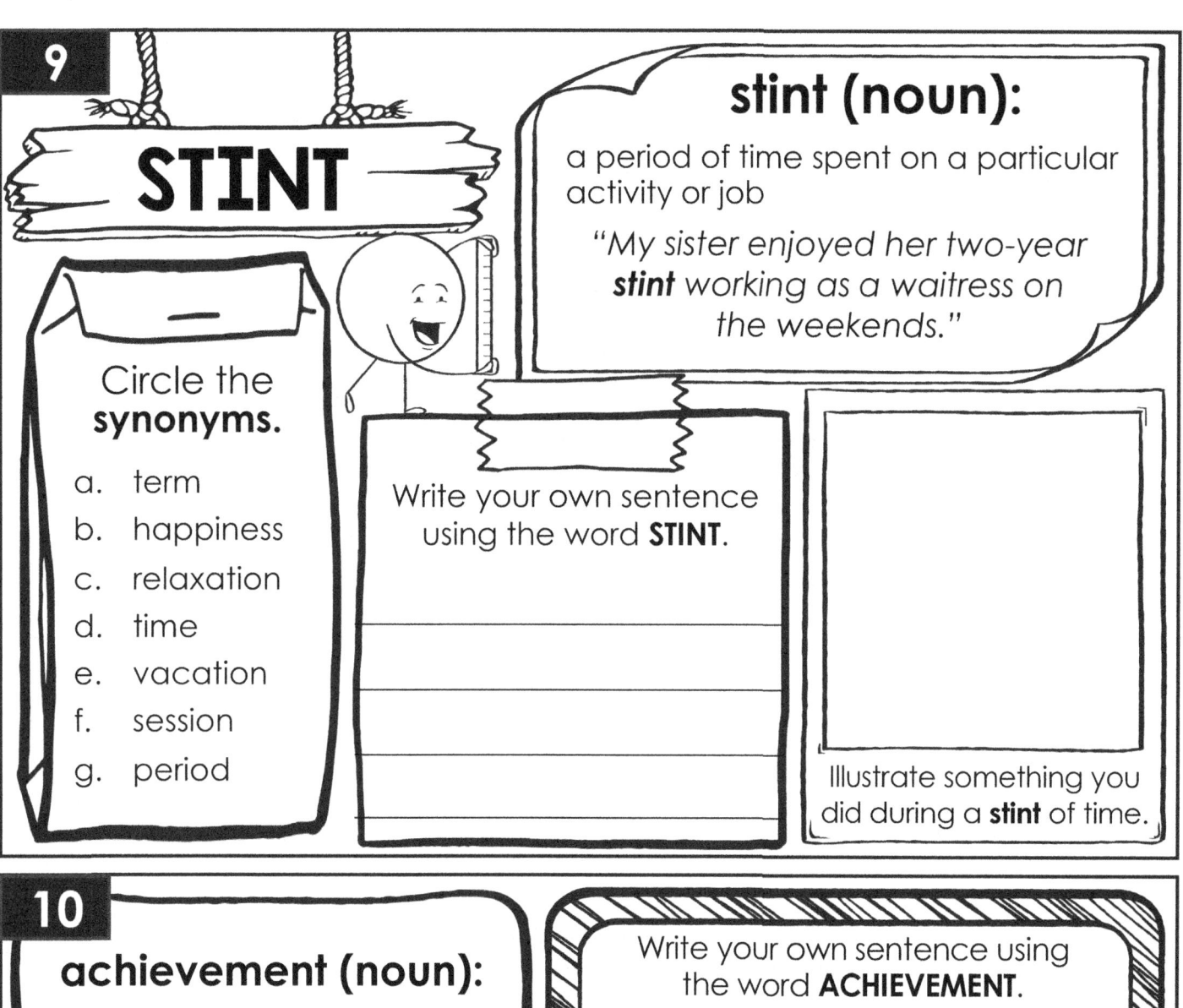

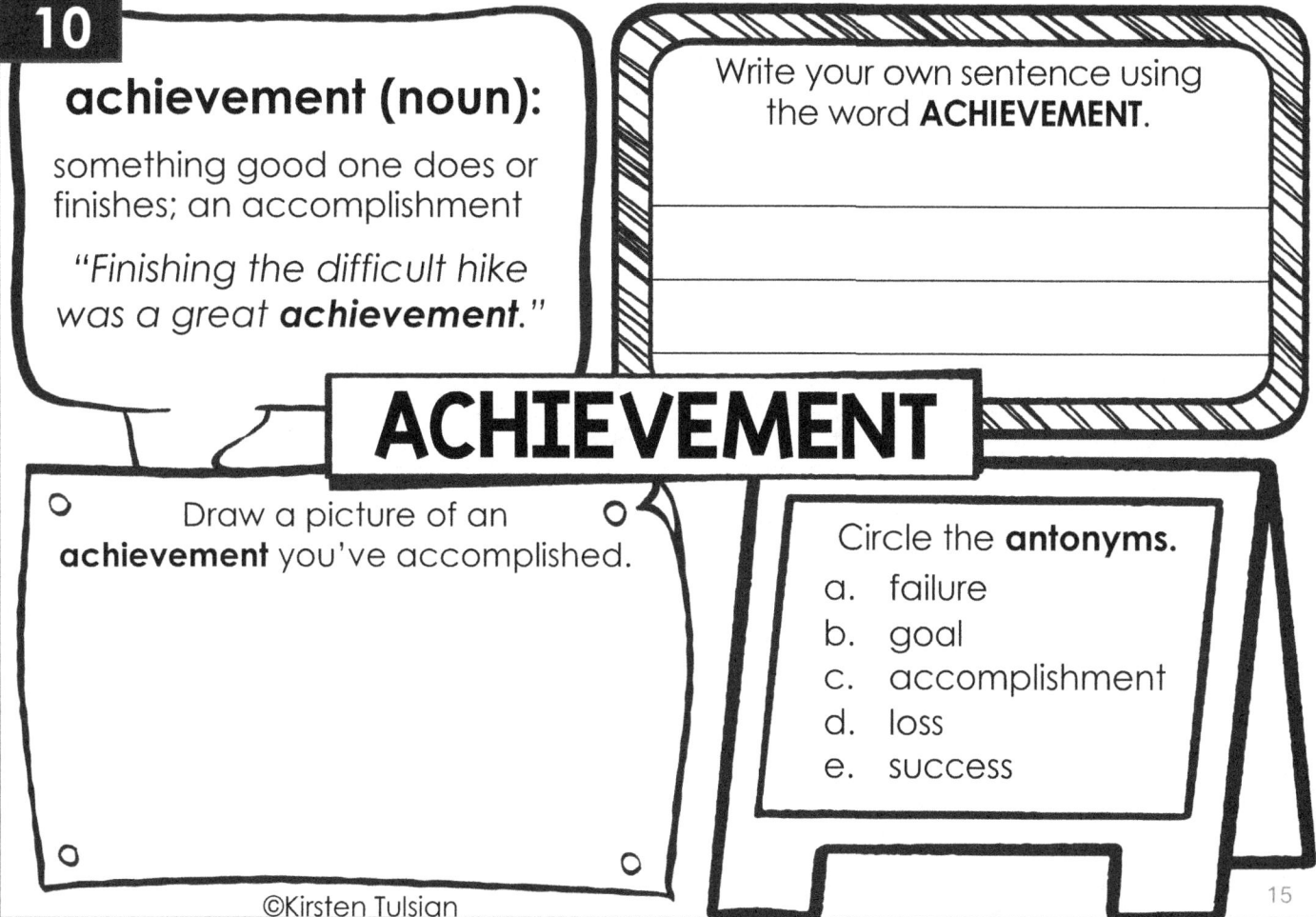

9 STINT

stint (noun): a period of time spent on a particular activity or job

*"My sister enjoyed her two-year **stint** working as a waitress on the weekends."*

Circle the **synonyms**.
a. term
b. happiness
c. relaxation
d. time
e. vacation
f. session
g. period

Write your own sentence using the word **STINT**.

Illustrate something you did during a **stint** of time.

10 ACHIEVEMENT

achievement (noun): something good one does or finishes; an accomplishment

*"Finishing the difficult hike was a great **achievement**."*

Write your own sentence using the word **ACHIEVEMENT**.

Draw a picture of an **achievement** you've accomplished.

Circle the **antonyms**.
a. failure
b. goal
c. accomplishment
d. loss
e. success

©Kirsten Tulsian

11

beneficial (adjective):
favorable or helpful; resulting in good

*"The vitamins I take each night are **beneficial** for my health."*

Make a list of three things you find **beneficial.**
1.
2.
3.

BENEFICIAL

Write your own sentence using the word **BENEFICIAL**.

Circle the **synonyms**.
a. helpful
b. useful
c. hurtful
d. valuable
e. harmful
f. worthless

12

profound (adjective):
very deep, meaningful, and important

*"Her beautiful painting had a **profound** impact on me."*

Choose the best word to replace **PROFOUND** in the sentence below.

My family experienced **profound** sadness when our dog passed away.

a. slight
b. deep
c. mild
d. minor

PROFOUND

Circle the **antonyms**.
a. deep
b. major
c. slight
d. mild
e. serious
f. minor

Write your own sentence using the word **PROFOUND**.

Illustrate something that deeply impacted you.

©Kirsten Tulsian

13

tranquil (adjective):

calm, peaceful, quiet; free from irritation or annoyance

"Lake Harriet is the most tranquil place in the entire city."

TRANQUIL

Draw a picture of the most **tranquil** place you've been.

Write your own sentence using the word **TRANQUIL**.

Circle the **synonyms.**
a. quiet
b. restful
c. rowdy
d. serene
e. noisy
f. undisturbed

14

ambitious (adjective):

having a desire to be successful, powerful, or famous

"He had an ambitious goal of starting his own business by the time he was 20 years old."

Choose the best word to replace **AMBITIOUS** in the sentence below.

Sima's **ambitious** goal to publish a book this year was successful!

a. boring   c. determined
b. annoying   d. easy

DOODLE IT!

AMBITIOUS

Write your own sentence using the word **AMBITIOUS**.

©Kirsten Tulsian

17

15

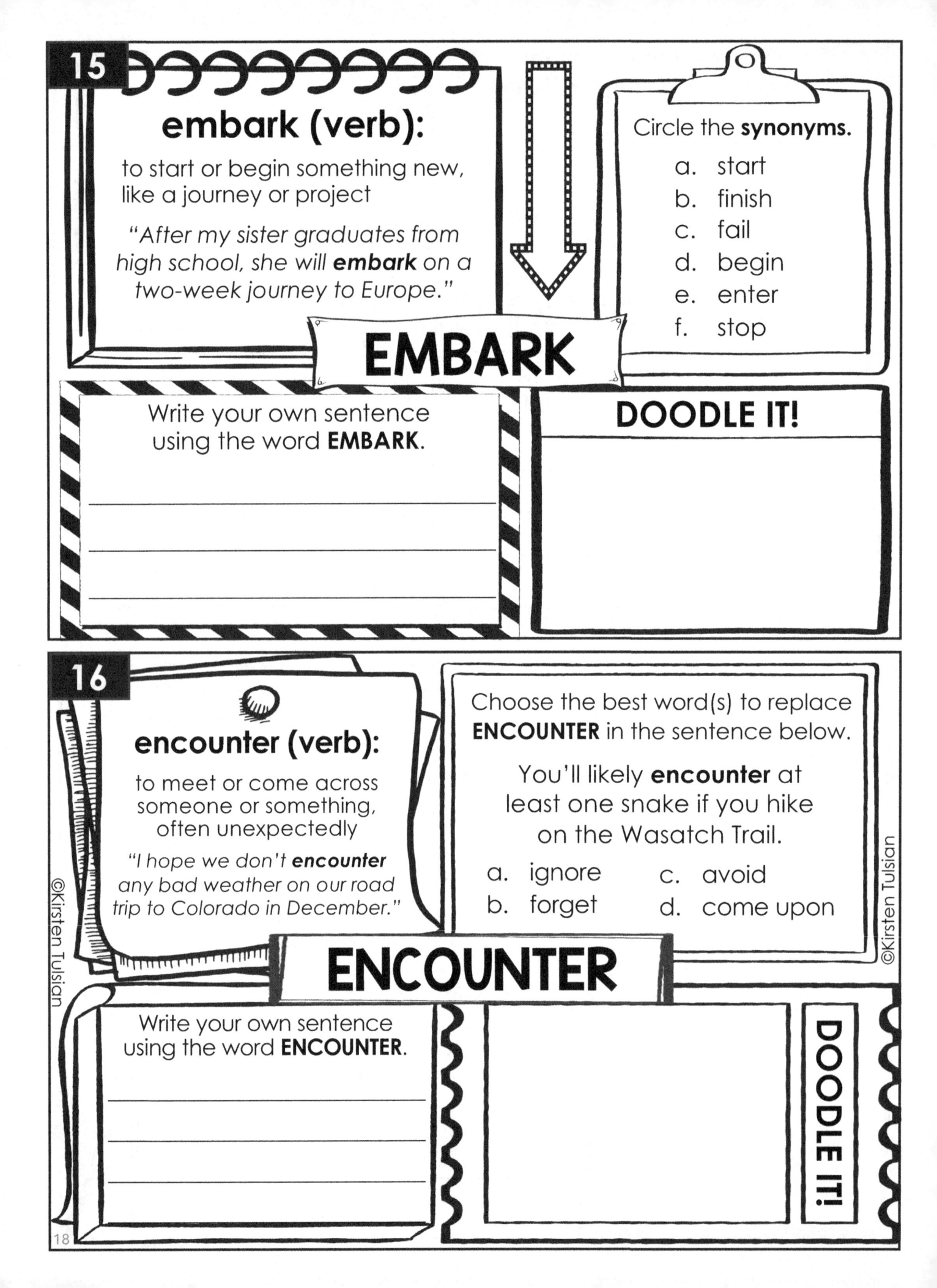

embark (verb):
to start or begin something new, like a journey or project

*"After my sister graduates from high school, she will **embark** on a two-week journey to Europe."*

EMBARK

Circle the **synonyms**.
a. start
b. finish
c. fail
d. begin
e. enter
f. stop

Write your own sentence using the word **EMBARK**.

DOODLE IT!

16

encounter (verb):
to meet or come across someone or something, often unexpectedly

*"I hope we don't **encounter** any bad weather on our road trip to Colorado in December."*

ENCOUNTER

Choose the best word(s) to replace **ENCOUNTER** in the sentence below.

You'll likely **encounter** at least one snake if you hike on the Wasatch Trail.

a. ignore
b. forget
c. avoid
d. come upon

Write your own sentence using the word **ENCOUNTER**.

DOODLE IT!

17 AVID

avid (adjective): being very enthusiastic or interested in something

"Although Annika likes nonfiction books, she is an **avid** reader of science fiction and fantasy."

Circle the **antonyms.**
a. unexcited
b. devoted
c. eager
d. dull
e. enthusiastic
f. uninterested
g. bored

Write your own sentence using the word **AVID**.

Illustrate something you feel enthusiastic about.

18 SCAVENGER

scavenger (noun): someone who looks for and collects things that others have thrown away or left behind

"My puppy is a **scavenger**, always looking for crumbs and scraps of food."

Write your own sentence using the word **SCAVENGER**.

Draw a picture of something you might find on a **SCAVENGER** hunt.

Circle the **synonyms.**
a. searcher
b. sleeper
c. gatherer
d. collector
e. actor

©Kirsten Tulsian

19

trivial (adjective):
not very important; not worth paying attention to

*"My problems seem **trivial** compared to my cousin, who just lost her cat."*

Draw a picture of something that might seem **trivial** to others but is important to you.

TRIVIAL

Write your own sentence using the word **TRIVIAL**.

Circle the **synonyms.**
a. minor
b. major
c. necessary
d. unimportant
e. useful
f. insignificant

20

boisterous (adjective):
noisy, lively, and full of energy; jolly

*"The **boisterous** fans cheered loudly when we won the game."*

Choose the best word to replace **BOISTEROUS** in the sentence below.

Although Sid is **boisterous**, he can be calm and quiet when necessary.
a. slow   c. uncomfortable
b. tired   d. energetic

BOISTEROUS

Circle the **antonyms.**
a. hyper
b. silent
c. calm
d. energetic
e. restrained
f. lively

Write your own sentence using the word **BOISTEROUS**.

DOODLE IT!

21

massive (adjective):

something very big or heavy; large in size, degree, or scale

"It will require a **massive** effort for him to remove the **massive** amount of trash in his room."

MASSIVE

DOODLE IT!

Write your own sentence using the word **MASSIVE**.

Choose the best word to replace **MASSIVE** in the sentence below.

If you have a **massive** amount of money, you can buy a yacht.

a. minimal
b. sizeable
c. tiny
d. small

22

grotesque (adjective):

strange, ugly, or unnatural in appearance; bizarre

"I created a **grotesque** self-portrait with oil paints."

Choose the best word to replace **GROTESQUE** in the sentence below.

He wore a **grotesque** monster mask as a part of his costume.

a. beautiful   c. normal
b. weird   d. cute

GROTESQUE

DOODLE IT!

Write your own sentence using the word **GROTESQUE**.

23

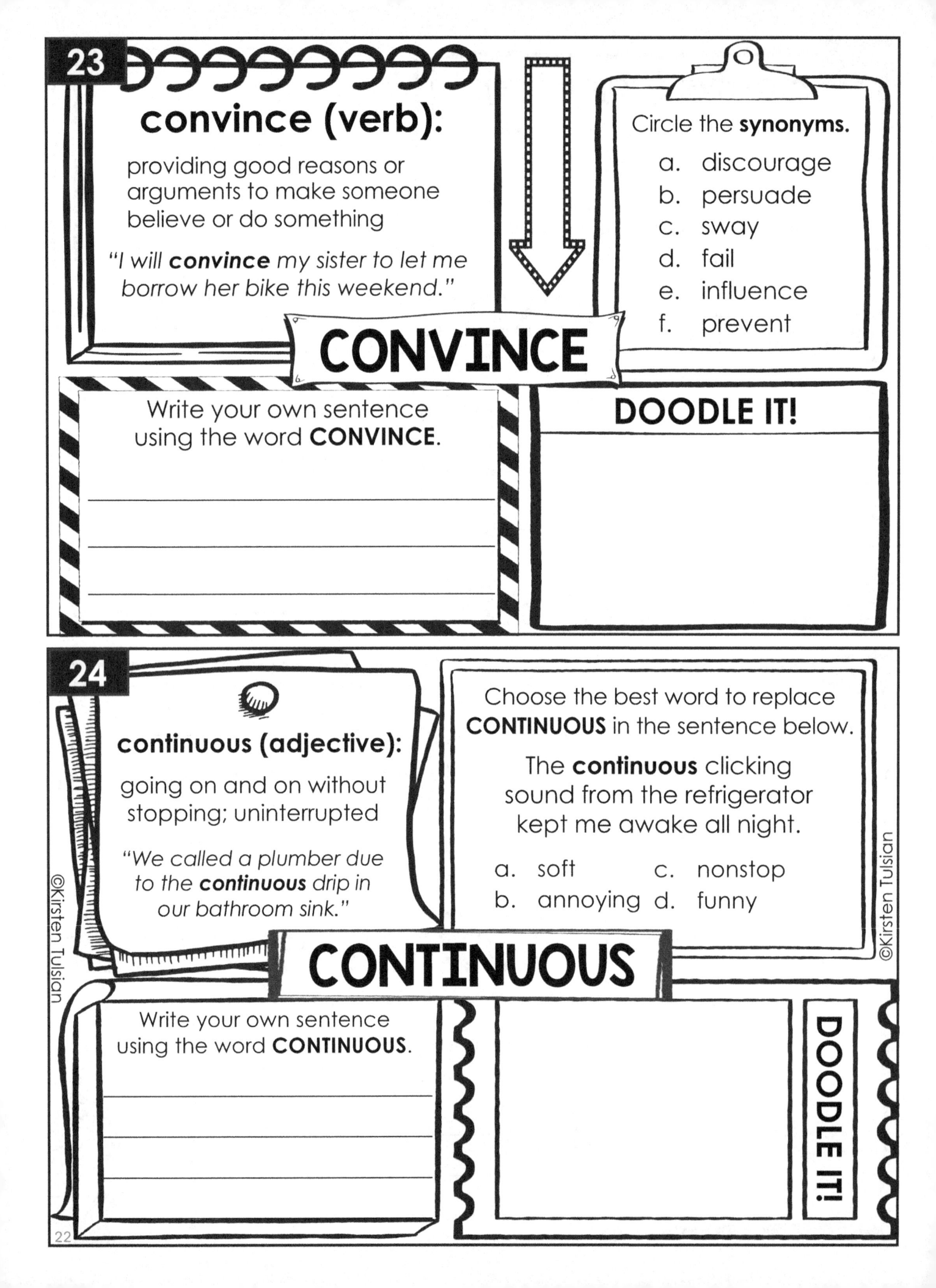

convince (verb):
providing good reasons or arguments to make someone believe or do something

*"I will **convince** my sister to let me borrow her bike this weekend."*

Circle the **synonyms**.
a. discourage
b. persuade
c. sway
d. fail
e. influence
f. prevent

CONVINCE

Write your own sentence using the word **CONVINCE**.

DOODLE IT!

24

continuous (adjective):
going on and on without stopping; uninterrupted

*"We called a plumber due to the **continuous** drip in our bathroom sink."*

Choose the best word to replace **CONTINUOUS** in the sentence below.

The **continuous** clicking sound from the refrigerator kept me awake all night.

a. soft
b. annoying
c. nonstop
d. funny

CONTINUOUS

Write your own sentence using the word **CONTINUOUS**.

DOODLE IT!

25 DECAY

decay (verb): breaking down, decomposing, or rotting

"After leaves fall from trees, they begin to **decay** as fungi, bacteria, and other organisms break them down."

Circle the **synonyms**.
a. grow
b. rot
c. crumble
d. build
e. develop
f. decompose
g. improve

Write your own sentence using the word **DECAY**.

DOODLE IT!

26 ACKNOWLEDGE

acknowledge (verb): to recognize, accept, or admit the truth or importance of something

"I **acknowledge** that I made a mistake and am sorry that I hurt your feelings."

Write your own sentence using the word **ACKNOWLEDGE**.

Draw a picture of something you **ACKNOWLEDGE** as a FACT OF LIFE.

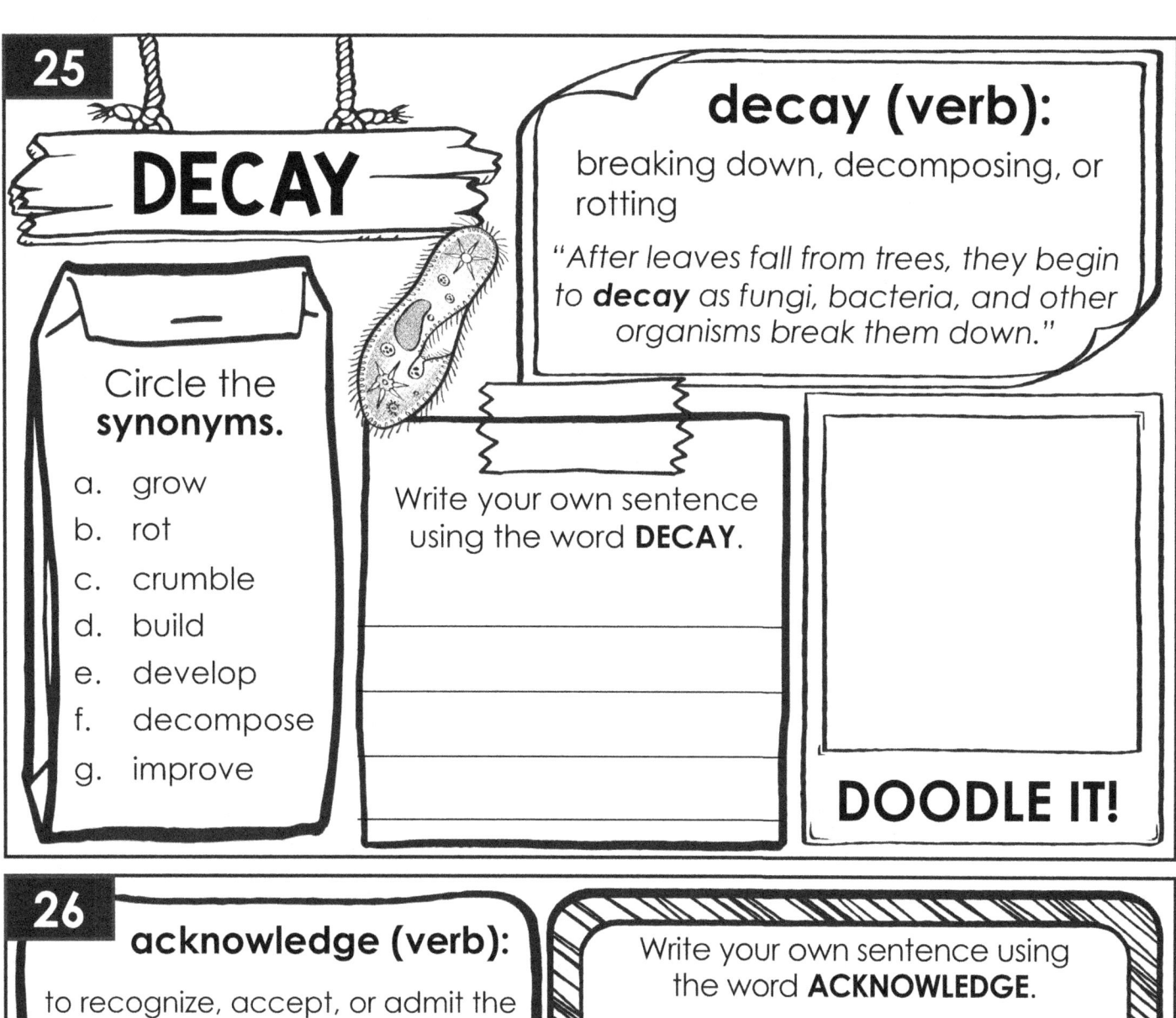

Circle the **antonyms**.
a. deny
b. disagree
c. accept
d. recognize
e. reject

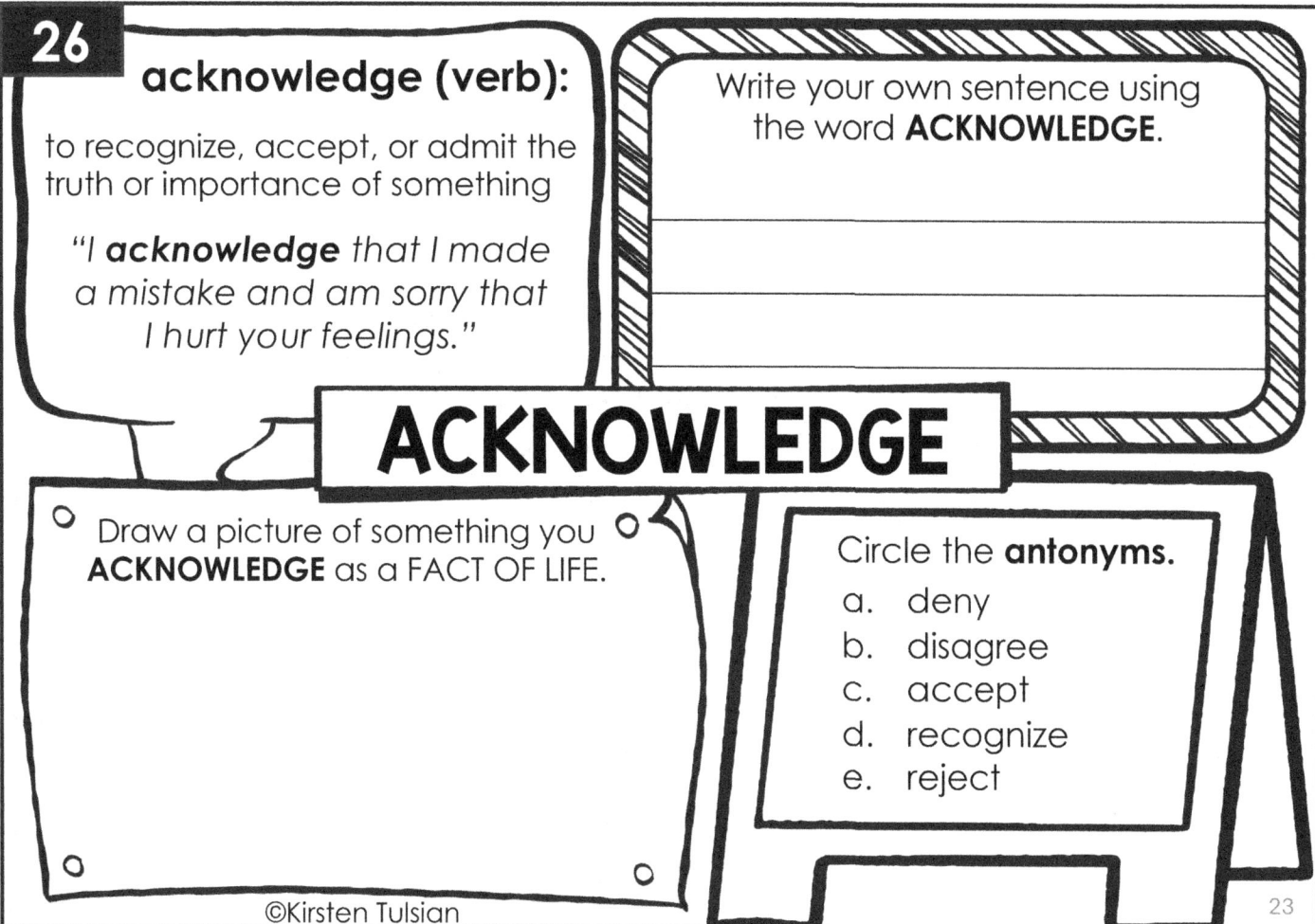

27

flustered (adjective):

in a state of nervous confusion, upset, or overwhelm

"I felt flustered when I walked into class after the bell rang."

Draw a picture of a time you felt **flustered**.

FLUSTERED

Write your own sentence using the word **FLUSTERED**.

Circle the **synonyms**.
a. calm
b. unsettled
c. bothered
d. agitated
e. peaceful
f. confident

28

astound (verb):

to shock or surprise someone when something amazing or unexpected happens

"The magician will astound the audience with her tricks."

Choose the best word to replace **ASTOUND** in the sentence below.

I will **astound** my cousins when I sing at our aunt's wedding.
a. bother   c. embarrass
b. amaze   d. criticize

ASTOUND

Write your own sentence using the word **ASTOUND**.

Create an illustration showing the last time you felt **astounded**.

29 venture (noun):

a risky or daring new journey, project, or undertaking

*"After our picnic in the park, we plan to **venture** into the dark woods by the lake's edge."*

Draw a picture of a **venture** you'd like to take in the future.

VENTURE

Write your own sentence using the word **VENTURE**.

Choose the best word to replace **VENTURE** in the sentence below.

Publishing my writing is a new **venture** for me.

a. storm
b. undertaking
c. race
d. plug

30 rejuvenate (verb):

to restore or give new energy; to make something look or feel healthy or young again

*"Relaxation and sleep can **rejuvenate** your body and mind."*

Choose the best word to replace **REJUVENATE** in the sentence below.

Rejuvenate the dying plant by watering it and placing it in direct sunlight.

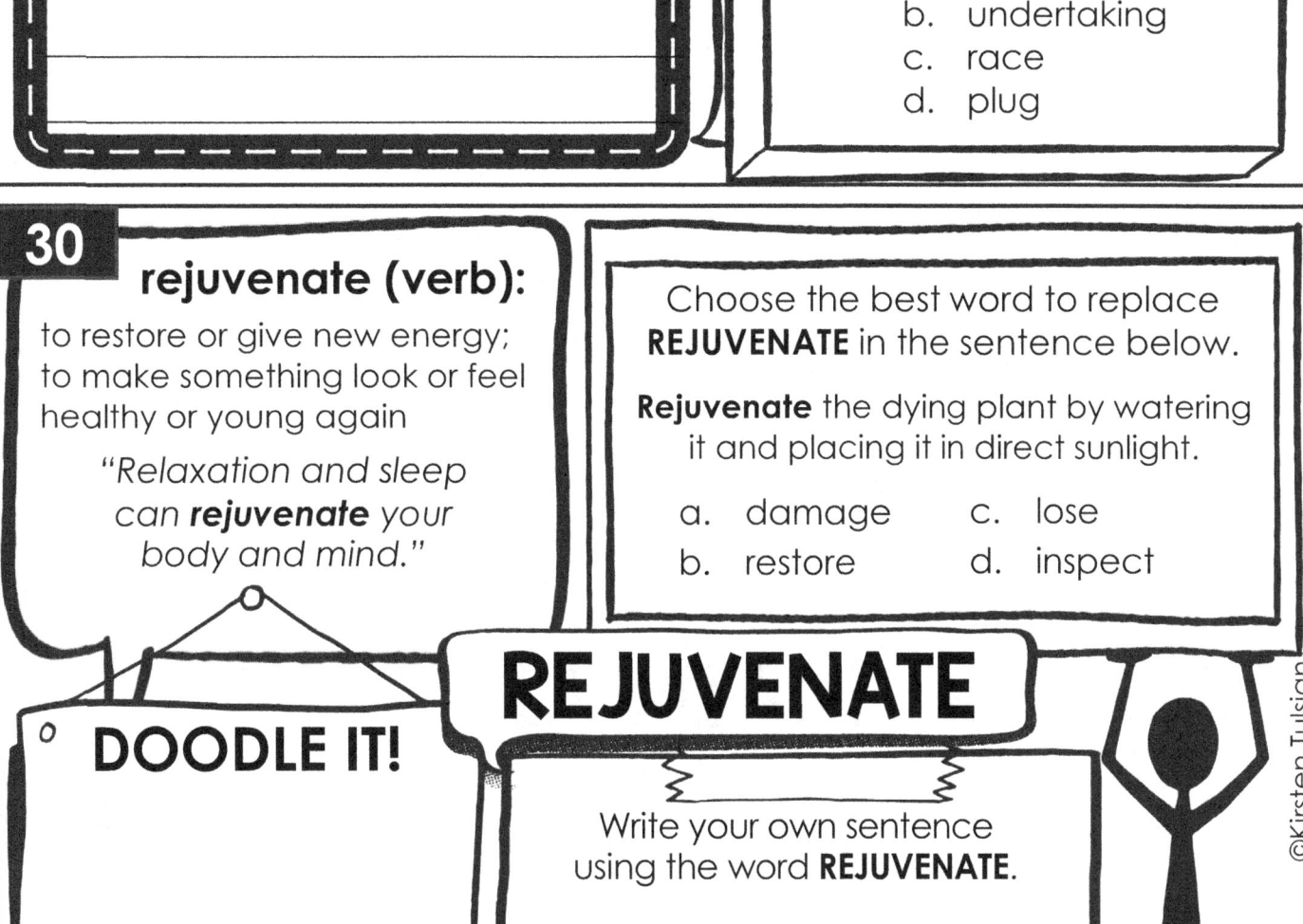

a. damage
b. restore
c. lose
d. inspect

DOODLE IT!

REJUVENATE

Write your own sentence using the word **REJUVENATE**.

©Kirsten Tulsian

31

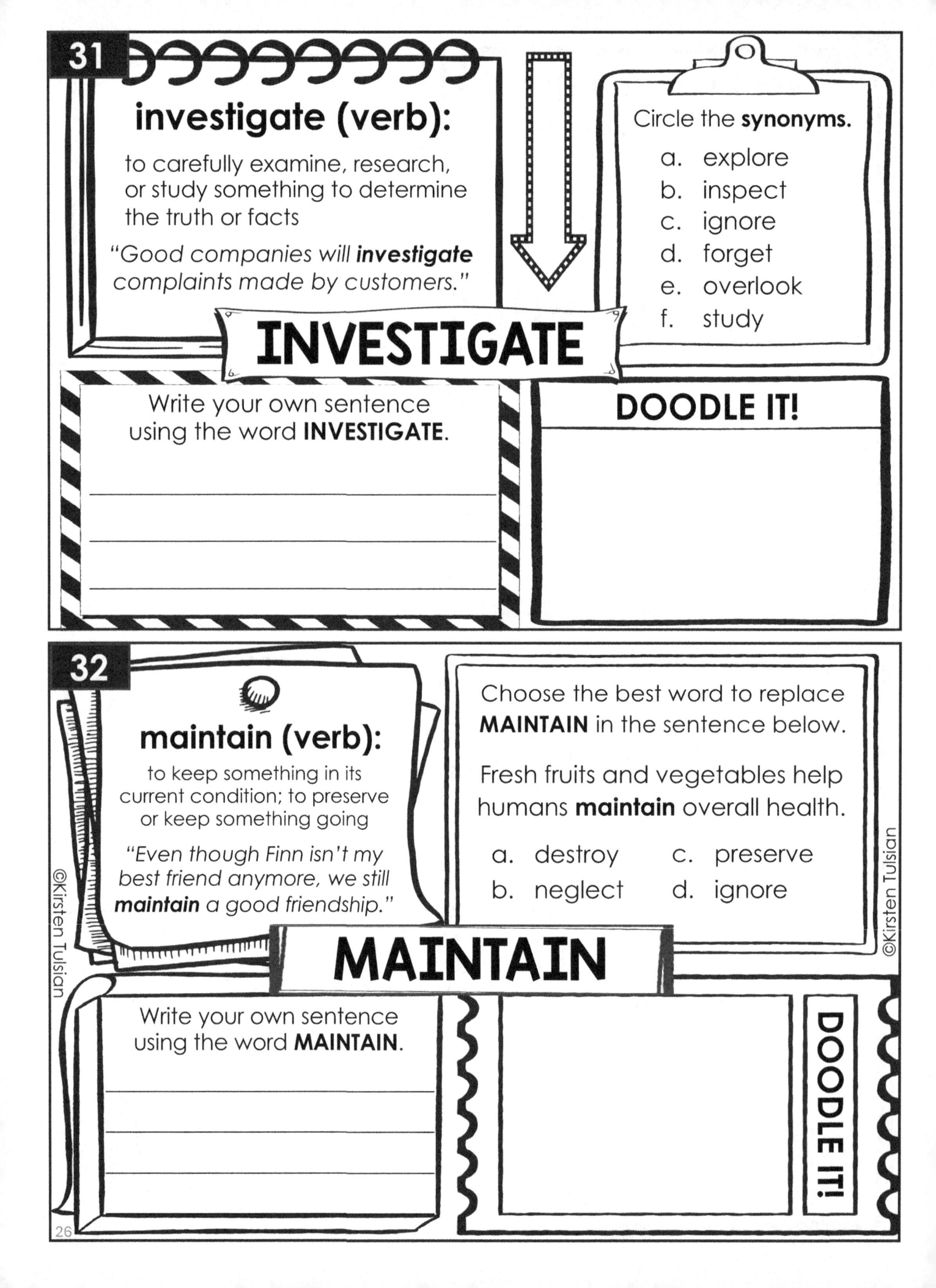

investigate (verb):
to carefully examine, research, or study something to determine the truth or facts

"Good companies will **investigate** complaints made by customers."

Circle the **synonyms**.
a. explore
b. inspect
c. ignore
d. forget
e. overlook
f. study

INVESTIGATE

Write your own sentence using the word **INVESTIGATE**.

DOODLE IT!

32

maintain (verb):
to keep something in its current condition; to preserve or keep something going

"Even though Finn isn't my best friend anymore, we still **maintain** a good friendship."

Choose the best word to replace **MAINTAIN** in the sentence below.

Fresh fruits and vegetables help humans **maintain** overall health.

a. destroy
b. neglect
c. preserve
d. ignore

MAINTAIN

Write your own sentence using the word **MAINTAIN**.

DOODLE IT!

33 ALOOF

aloof (adjective): unfriendly or distant (either physically or emotionally); reserved

"I am friendly but might appear aloof around new people because I'm a little bit shy."

Circle the **synonyms.**

a. distant
b. social
c. withdrawn
d. unsociable
e. reserved
f. friendly
g. outgoing

Write your own sentence using the word **ALOOF**.

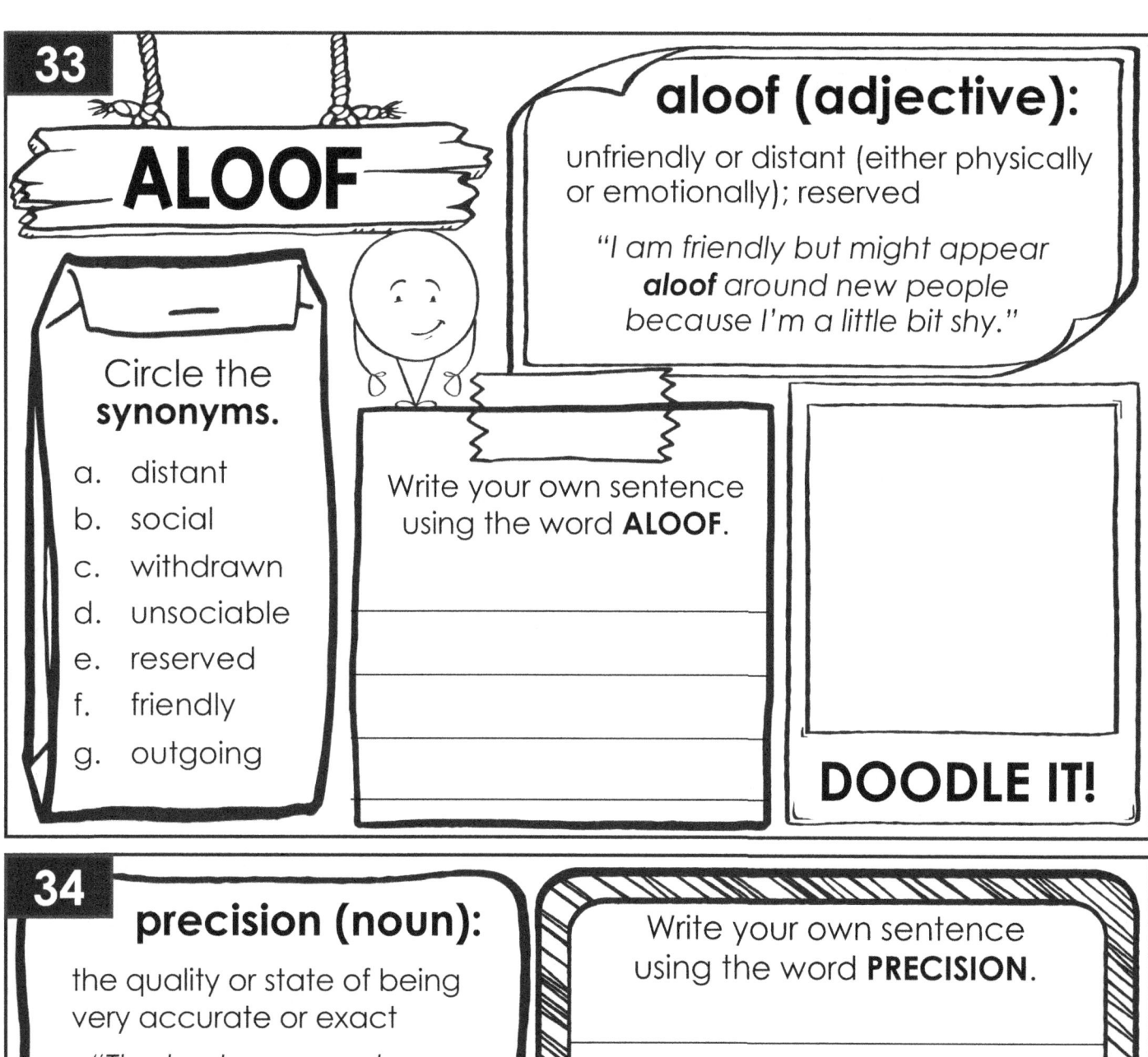

DOODLE IT!

34 PRECISION

precision (noun): the quality or state of being very accurate or exact

"The best surgeons have mastered precision, knowledge, and quality."

Write your own sentence using the word **PRECISION**.

Make a list of three things that require **precision** to be successful.

1.
2.
3.

Circle the **antonyms.**

a. accuracy
b. inaccuracy
c. perfection
d. guesswork
e. carefulness

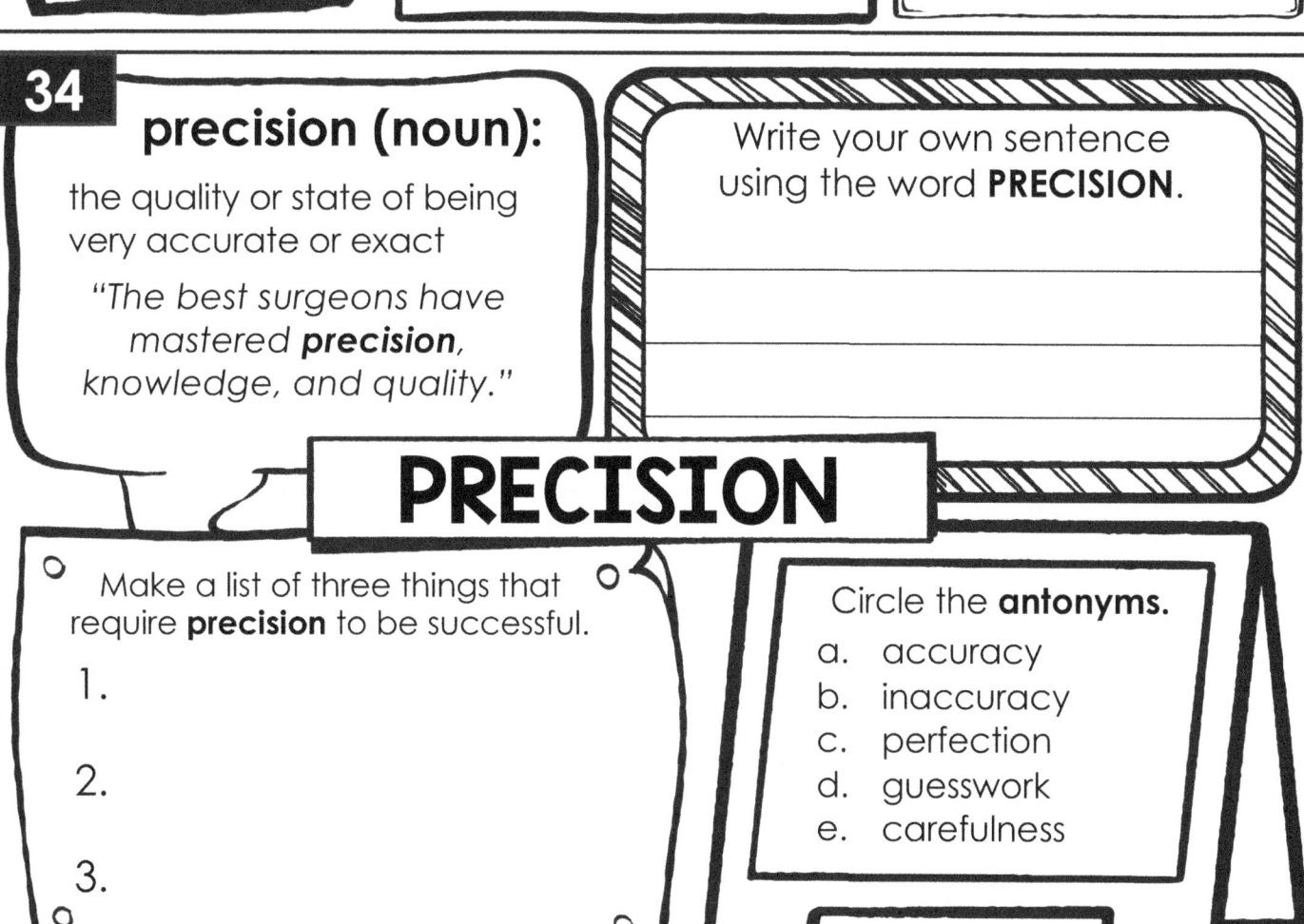

©Kirsten Tulsian

35

remorse (noun):
guilt, sadness, or regret about a choice or behavior

*"I would forgive you if you showed **remorse** for your actions."*

Draw a picture of a time when you felt **remorse** about something.

REMORSE

Write your own sentence using the word **REMORSE**.

Circle the **synonyms**.
a. sorrow
b. peace
c. regret
d. shame
e. understanding
f. guilt

36

predict (verb):
to say something you think will happen in the future

*"I **predict** we will win the championship soccer game."*

Choose the best word to replace **PREDICT** in the sentence below.

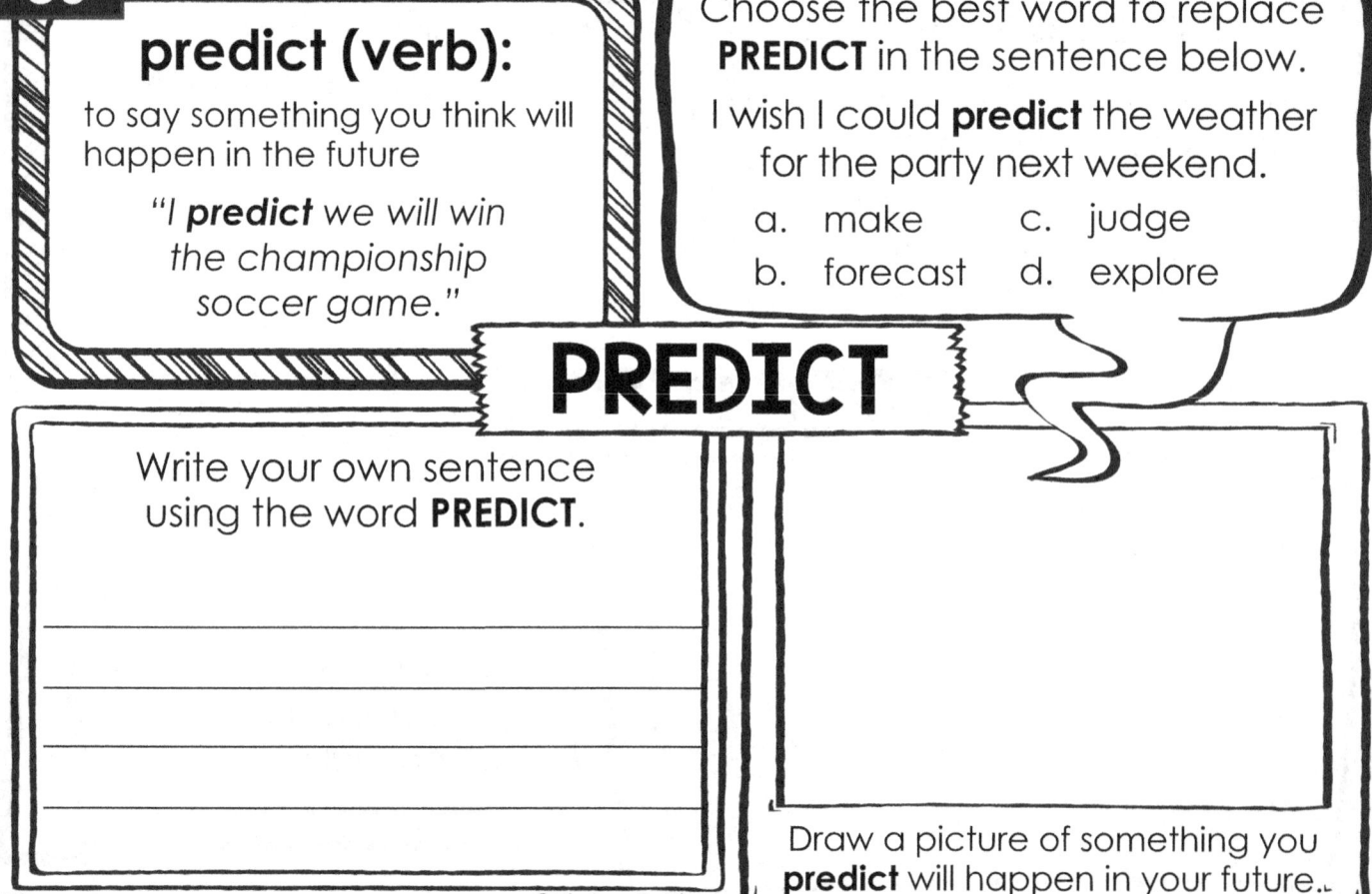

I wish I could **predict** the weather for the party next weekend.
a. make   c. judge
b. forecast   d. explore

PREDICT

Write your own sentence using the word **PREDICT**.

Draw a picture of something you **predict** will happen in your future.

37 bizarre (adjective):

strikingly unusual or odd, often in an interesting or amusing way

*"The book had a **bizarre** series of twists at the end."*

BIZARRE

Draw a picture of something **bizarre** that's happened to you.

Write your own sentence using the word **BIZARRE**.

Circle the **synonyms.**
a. reasonable
b. absurd
c. crazy
d. likely
e. strange
f. normal

38 discreet (adjective):

being thoughtful and careful in what you say and do, especially to avoid embarrassing yourself or others or to keep a secret

*"I made a **discreet** exit because I didn't want to wake the baby."*

Choose the best word to replace **DISCREET** in the sentence below.

Her party is a surprise, so please be **discreet** when she mentions her birthday.

a. bold
b. careless
c. direct
d. cautious

DOODLE IT!

DISCREET

Write your own sentence using the word **DISCREET**.

39

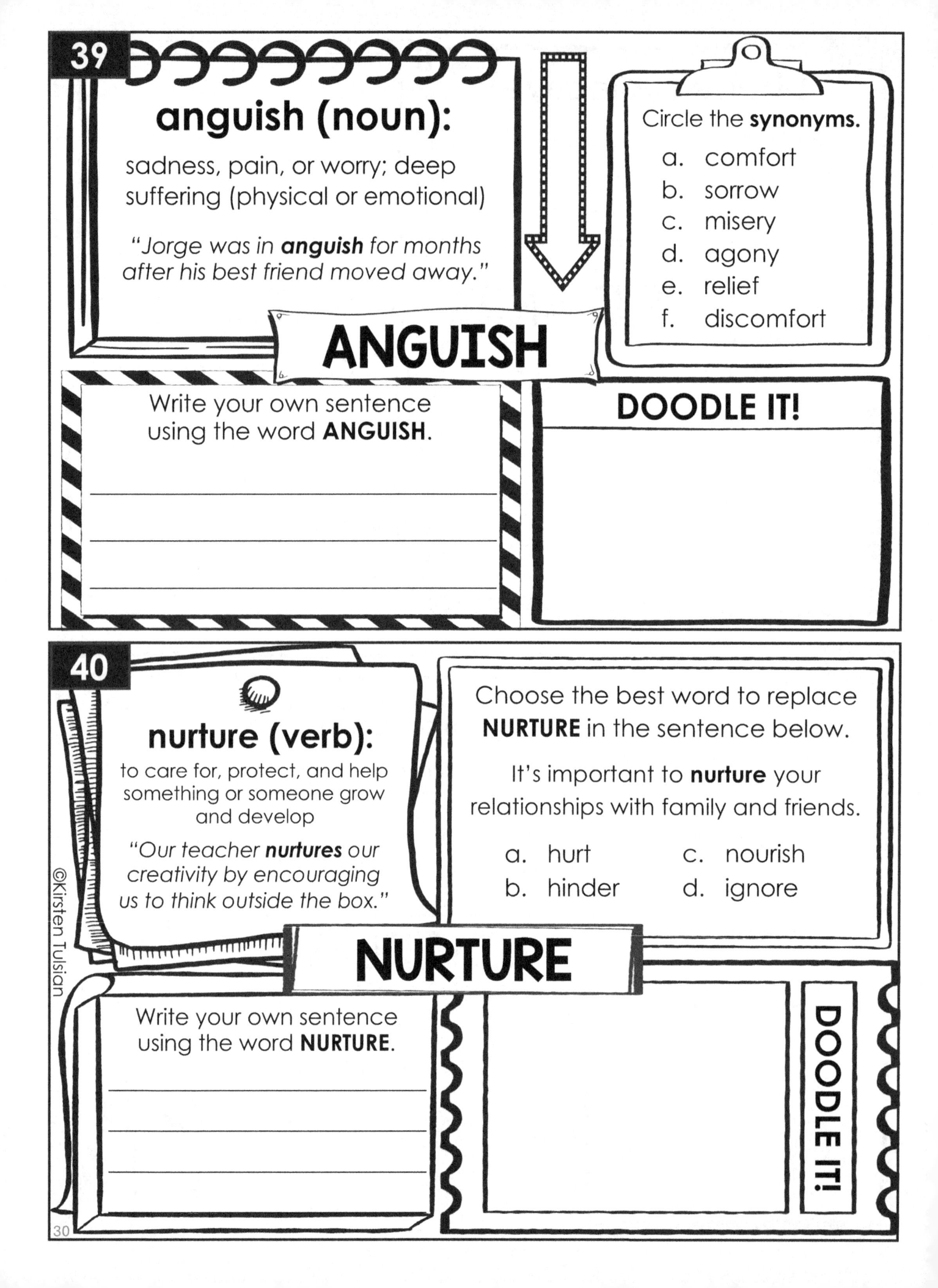

anguish (noun):

sadness, pain, or worry; deep suffering (physical or emotional)

*"Jorge was in **anguish** for months after his best friend moved away."*

Circle the synonyms.
a. comfort
b. sorrow
c. misery
d. agony
e. relief
f. discomfort

ANGUISH

Write your own sentence using the word **ANGUISH**.

DOODLE IT!

40

nurture (verb):

to care for, protect, and help something or someone grow and develop

*"Our teacher **nurtures** our creativity by encouraging us to think outside the box."*

Choose the best word to replace **NURTURE** in the sentence below.

It's important to **nurture** your relationships with family and friends.

a. hurt
b. hinder
c. nourish
d. ignore

NURTURE

Write your own sentence using the word **NURTURE**.

DOODLE IT!

©Kirsten Tulsian

41 BLAND

bland (adjective):
dull, boring, or without much flavor or excitement

"The **bland** soup will taste better if you add more spices."

Circle the **synonyms.**
a. boring
b. exciting
c. delicious
d. drab
e. uninteresting
f. interesting
g. powerful

Write your own sentence using the word **BLAND**.

DOODLE IT!

42

obnoxious (adjective):
very rude, unpleasant, or annoying, causing others to feel upset or bothered

"The **obnoxious** chirping sound from the smoke alarm woke us up in the middle of the night."

Write your own sentence using the word **OBNOXIOUS**.

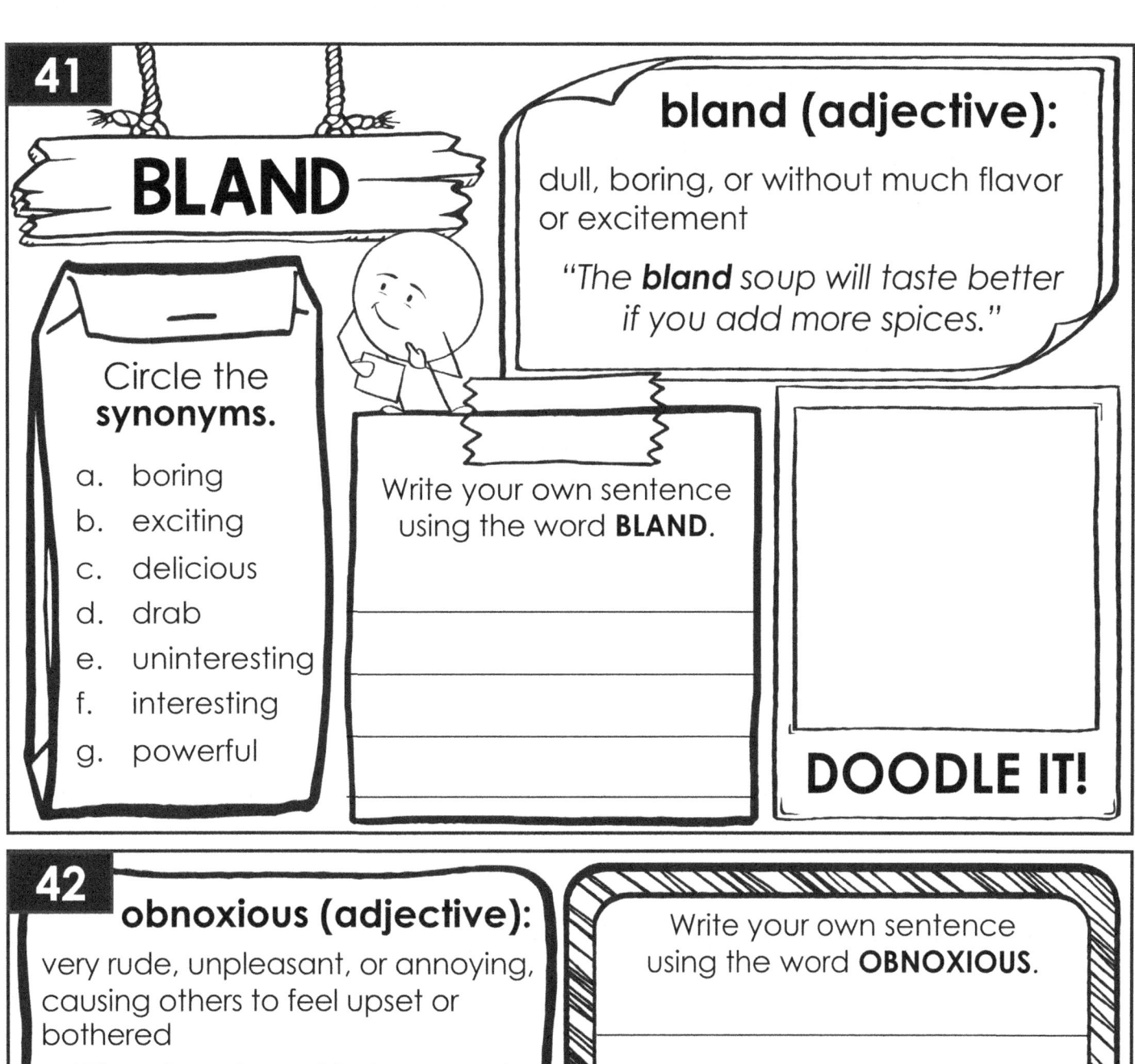

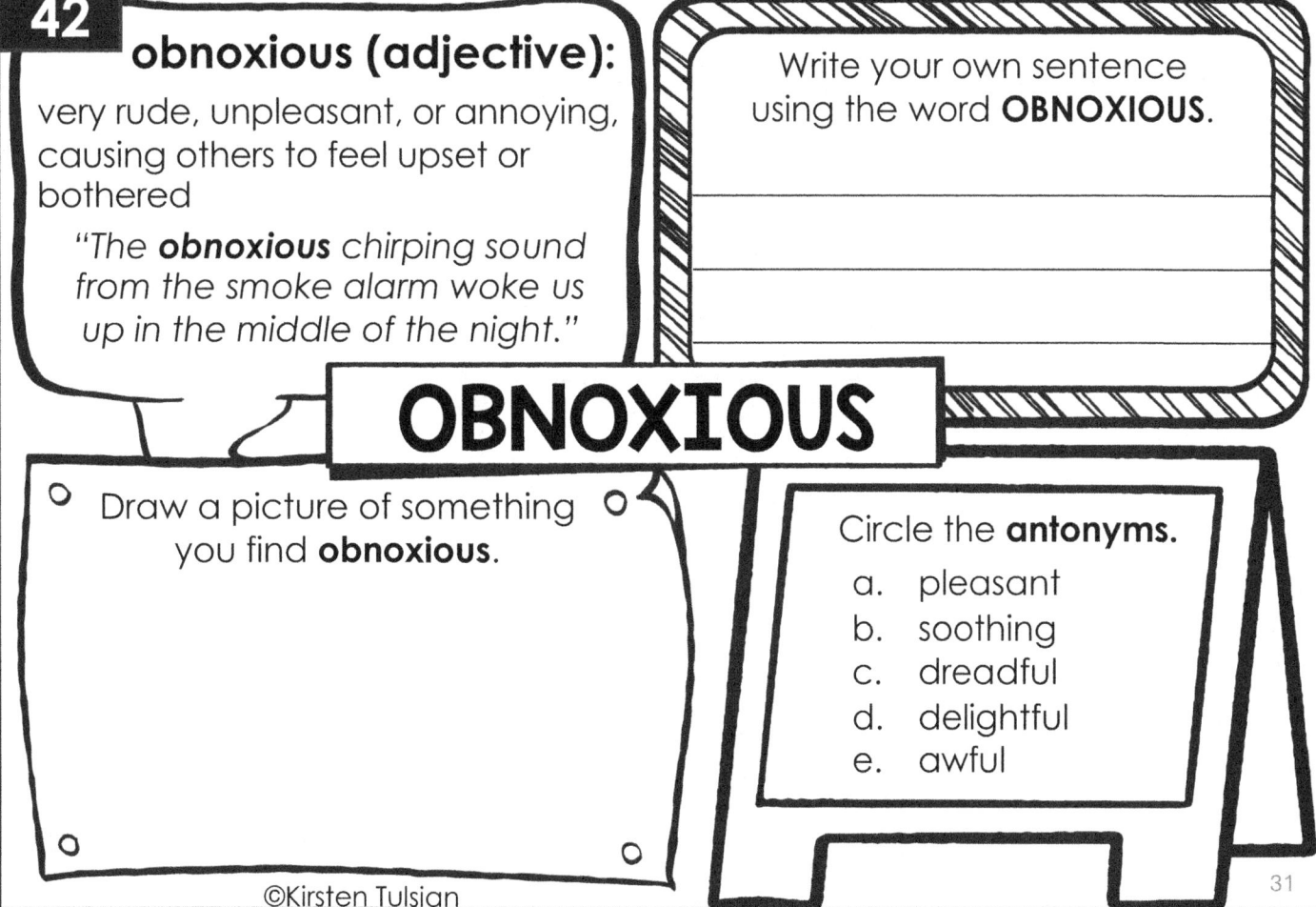

OBNOXIOUS

Draw a picture of something you find **obnoxious**.

Circle the **antonyms.**
a. pleasant
b. soothing
c. dreadful
d. delightful
e. awful

©Kirsten Tulsian

43

rigorous (adjective):

thorough, strict, or accurate; with great attention to detail

"Some dog breeds require **rigorous** daily exercise."

Write about the most **rigorous** test you've ever taken.

RIGOROUS

Write your own sentence using the word **RIGOROUS**.

Circle the **synonyms**.
a. easy
b. hard
c. gentle
d. strict
e. accurate
f. mild

44

disgruntled (adjective):

unhappy, annoyed, angry, or dissatisfied

"The **disgruntled** passengers had been waiting for their flight to leave for six hours."

Choose the best word to replace **DISGRUNTLED** in the sentence below.

Martha was **disgruntled** after she got terrible service at the restaurant.

a. frustrated   c. satisfied
b. bored   d. pleased

DISGRUNTLED

Circle the **antonyms**.
a. glad
b. happy
c. upset
d. miserable
e. joyful
f. disturbed

Write your own sentence using the word **DISGRUNTLED**.

DOODLE IT!

©Kirsten Tulsian

45 efficient (adjective):

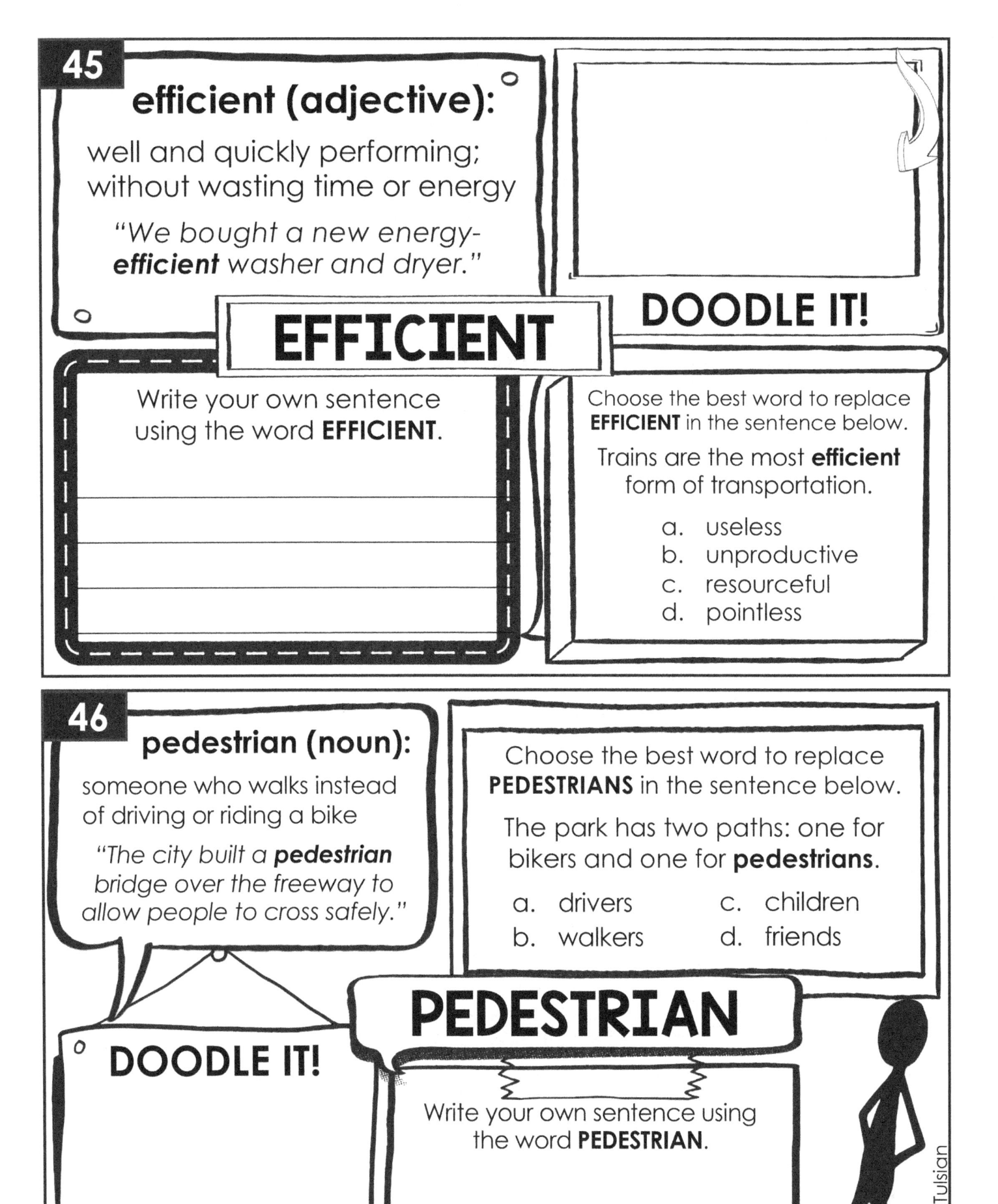

well and quickly performing; without wasting time or energy

*"We bought a new energy-**efficient** washer and dryer."*

EFFICIENT

DOODLE IT!

Write your own sentence using the word **EFFICIENT**.

Choose the best word to replace **EFFICIENT** in the sentence below.

Trains are the most **efficient** form of transportation.

- a. useless
- b. unproductive
- c. resourceful
- d. pointless

46 pedestrian (noun):

someone who walks instead of driving or riding a bike

*"The city built a **pedestrian** bridge over the freeway to allow people to cross safely."*

Choose the best word to replace **PEDESTRIANS** in the sentence below.

The park has two paths: one for bikers and one for **pedestrians**.

- a. drivers
- b. walkers
- c. children
- d. friends

DOODLE IT!

PEDESTRIAN

Write your own sentence using the word **PEDESTRIAN**.

©Kirsten Tulsian

47

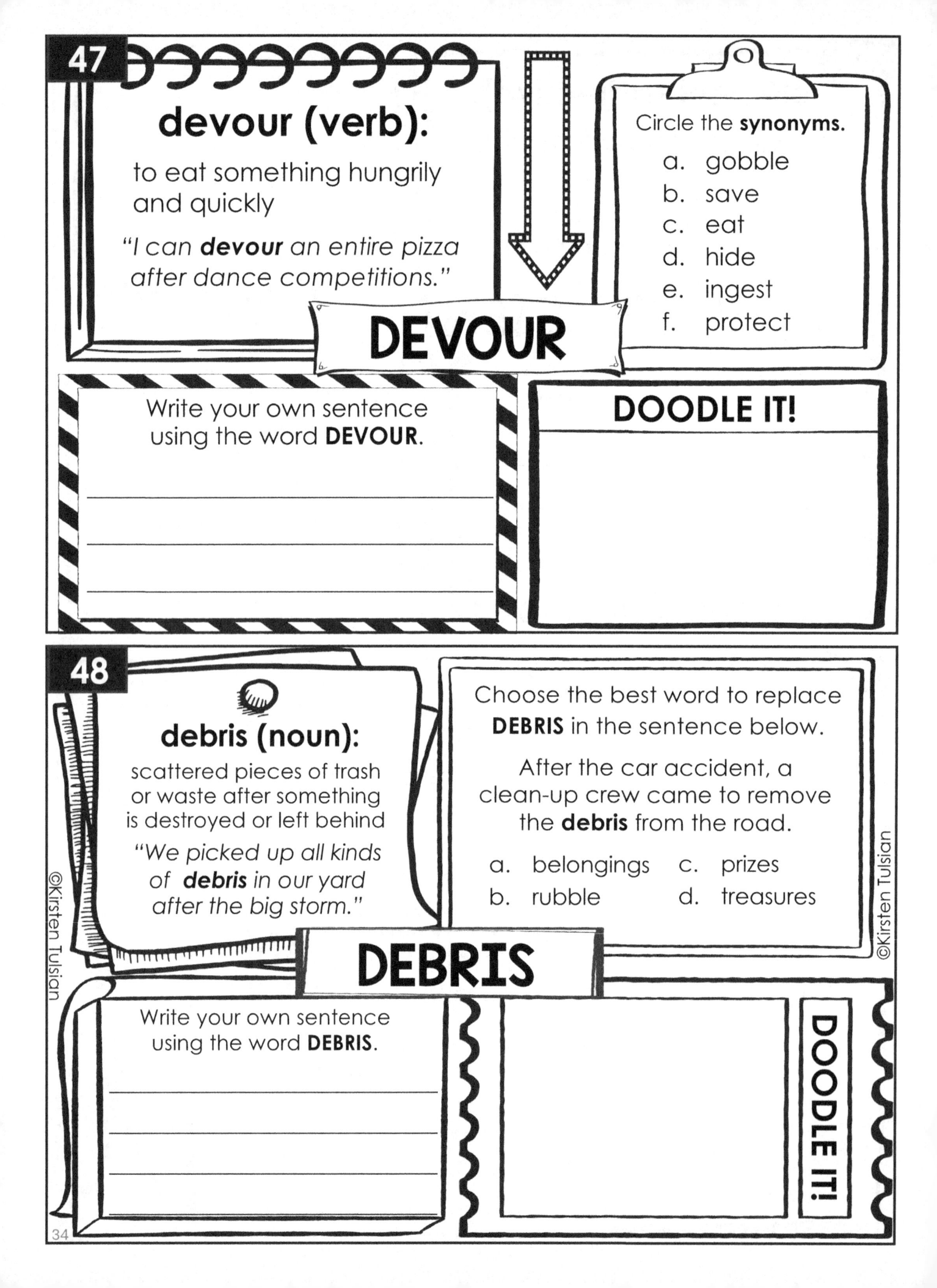

devour (verb):

to eat something hungrily and quickly

"I can **devour** an entire pizza after dance competitions."

DEVOUR

Circle the **synonyms**.
a. gobble
b. save
c. eat
d. hide
e. ingest
f. protect

Write your own sentence using the word **DEVOUR**.

DOODLE IT!

48

debris (noun):

scattered pieces of trash or waste after something is destroyed or left behind

"We picked up all kinds of **debris** in our yard after the big storm."

DEBRIS

Choose the best word to replace **DEBRIS** in the sentence below.

After the car accident, a clean-up crew came to remove the **debris** from the road.

a. belongings   c. prizes
b. rubble   d. treasures

Write your own sentence using the word **DEBRIS**.

DOODLE IT!

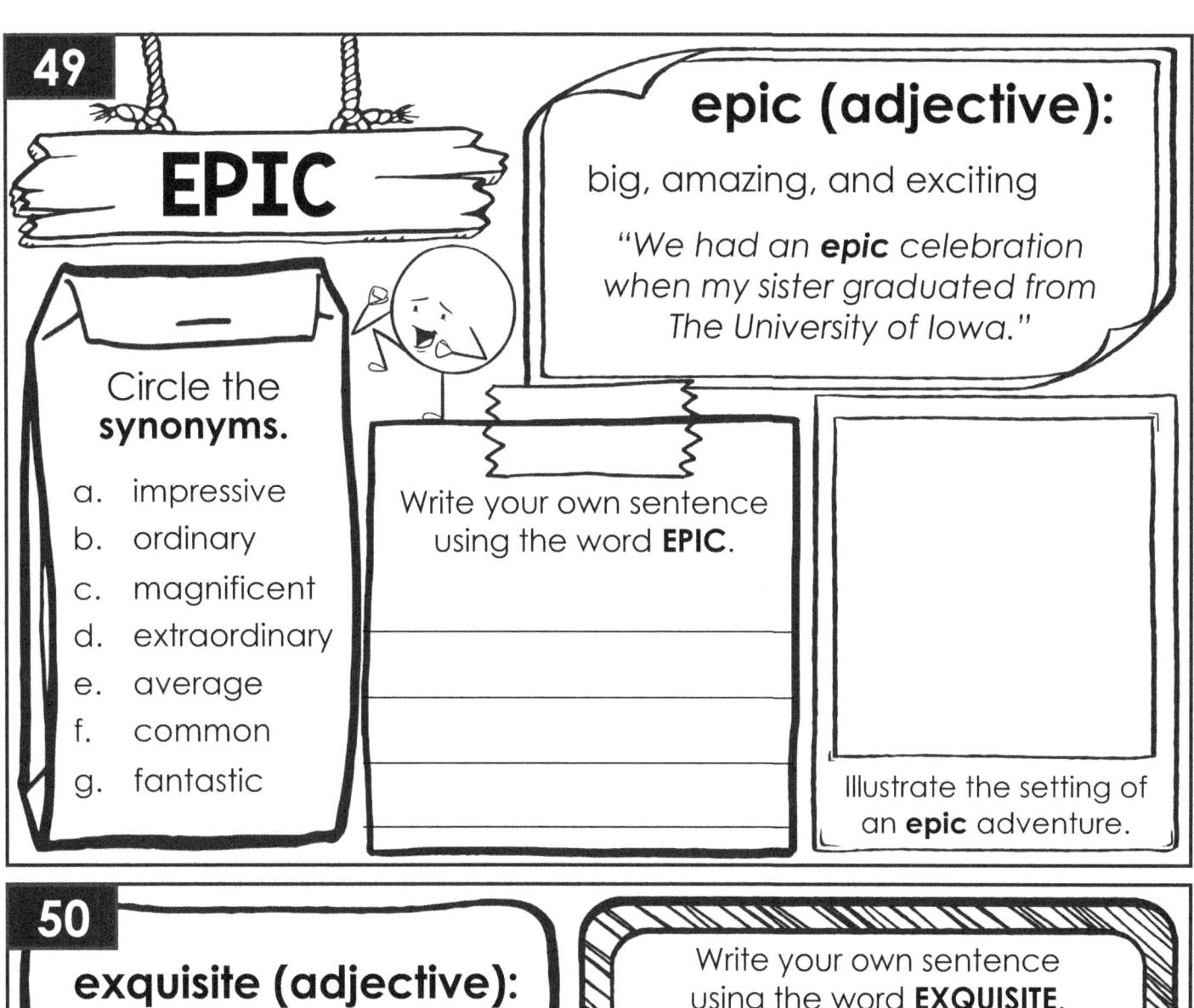

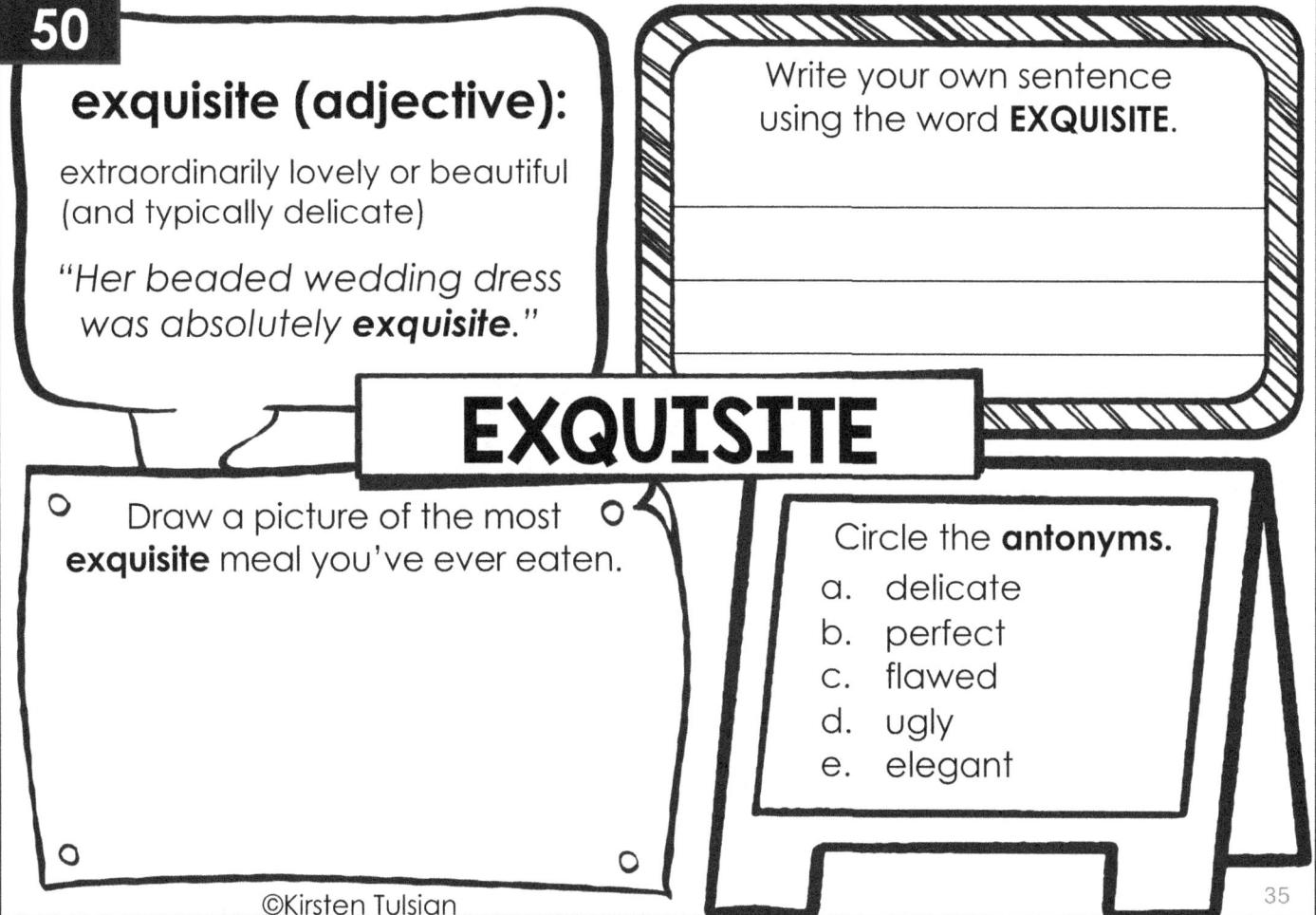

49 EPIC

epic (adjective):

big, amazing, and exciting

"We had an **epic** celebration when my sister graduated from The University of Iowa."

Circle the **synonyms.**

a. impressive
b. ordinary
c. magnificent
d. extraordinary
e. average
f. common
g. fantastic

Write your own sentence using the word **EPIC**.

Illustrate the setting of an **epic** adventure.

50 EXQUISITE

exquisite (adjective):

extraordinarily lovely or beautiful (and typically delicate)

"Her beaded wedding dress was absolutely **exquisite**."

Write your own sentence using the word **EXQUISITE**.

Draw a picture of the most **exquisite** meal you've ever eaten.

Circle the **antonyms.**

a. delicate
b. perfect
c. flawed
d. ugly
e. elegant

©Kirsten Tulsian

51

potential (noun):

the ability to develop, achieve, or succeed

"My little sister has the **potential** to be an Olympic gymnast."

List three areas in life where you hope to reach your **potential**.

1.
2.
3.

POTENTIAL

Write your own sentence using the word **POTENTIAL**.

Circle the **synonyms**.
a. inability
b. incompetence
c. ability
d. capability
e. weakness
f. power

52

awkward (adjective):

clumsy or ungraceful; causing embarrassment

"It was so **awkward** when I laughed and then snorted loudly in class."

Choose the best word to replace **AWKWARD** in the sentence below.

There was an **awkward** silence after Mrs. Hall asked who broke the glass.
a. gentle   c. uncomfortable
b. kind   d. peaceful

AWKWARD

Circle the **antonyms**.
a. graceful
b. confident
c. clumsy
d. calm
e. ungraceful
f. embarrassed

Write your own sentence using the word **AWKWARD**.

DOODLE IT!

53 immense (adjective):

huge or vast; marked by greatness in size or degree

*"The ocean is so **immense**; it looks like it goes on forever."*

IMMENSE

Draw a picture of something you have **immense** gratitude for.

Write your own sentence using the word **IMMENSE**.

Circle the **synonyms**.
a. gigantic
b. small
c. massive
d. miniature
e. little
f. enormous

54 beckon (verb):

to gesture or wave with a hand, arm, or head to encourage someone to come closer or follow

*"The teacher **beckoned** Nina to the front of the room when it was her turn to share."*

Choose the best word(s) to replace **BECKONED** in the sentence below.

Manny **beckoned** Charlotte to walk home with him after school.

a. motioned   c. froze
b. screamed at   d. refused

DOODLE IT!

BECKON

Write your own sentence using the word **BECKON**.

©Kirsten Tulsian

55

suitable (adjective):

good or right for a particular purpose or situation

*"This book is **suitable** for kids younger than 14 years old."*

SUITABLE

Circle the **synonyms**.
a. fitting
b. improper
c. appropriate
d. acceptable
e. useless
f. incorrect

Write your own sentence using the word **SUITABLE**.

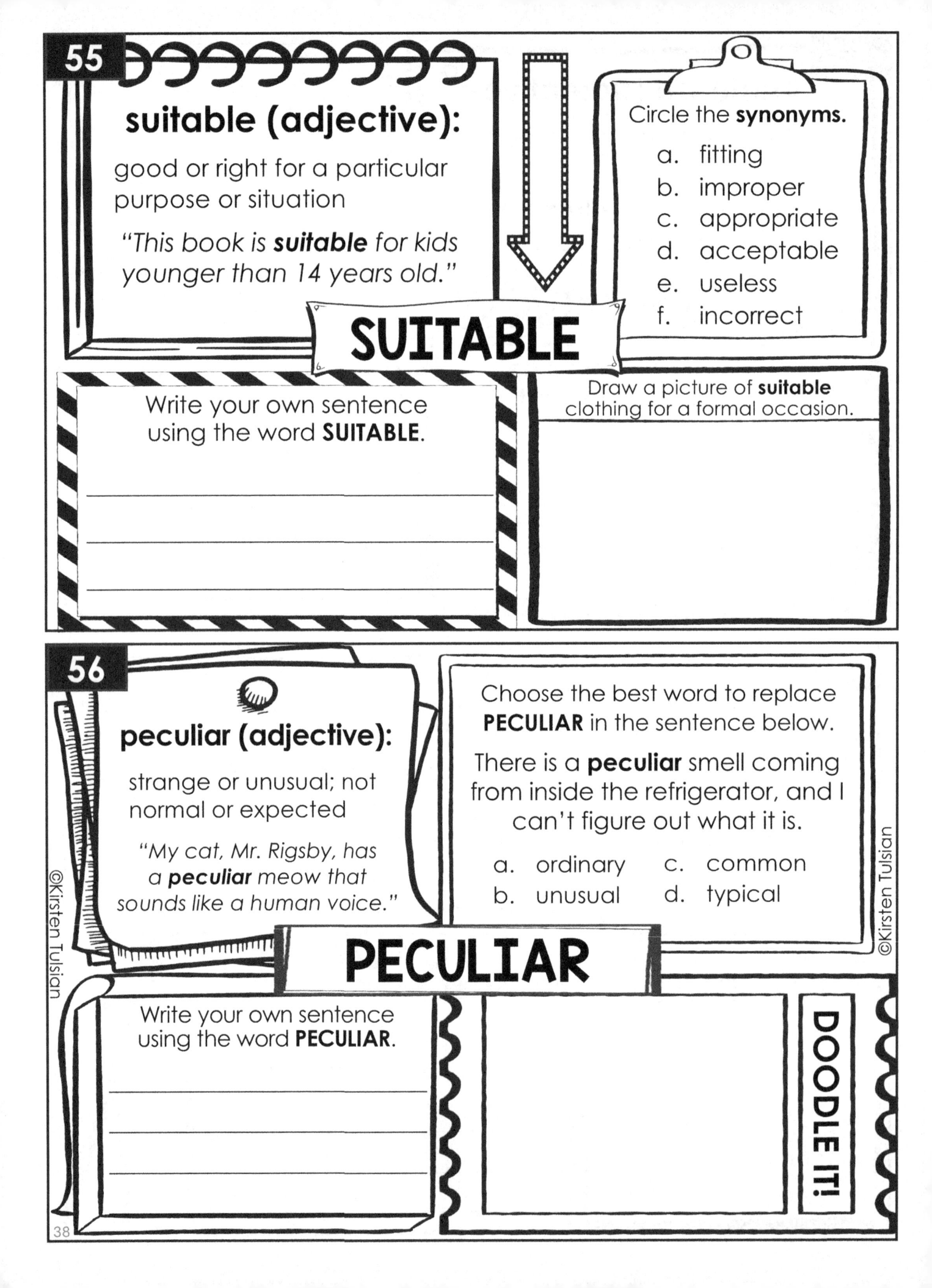

Draw a picture of **suitable** clothing for a formal occasion.

56

peculiar (adjective):

strange or unusual; not normal or expected

*"My cat, Mr. Rigsby, has a **peculiar** meow that sounds like a human voice."*

PECULIAR

Choose the best word to replace **PECULIAR** in the sentence below.

There is a **peculiar** smell coming from inside the refrigerator, and I can't figure out what it is.

a. ordinary   c. common
b. unusual   d. typical

Write your own sentence using the word **PECULIAR**.

DOODLE IT!

57 ABRUPT

abrupt (adjective): happening surprisingly suddenly or unexpectedly

"After the **abrupt** change in weather, we decided not to go for a hike."

Circle the **antonyms.**

a. quick
b. expected
c. unforeseen
d. predicted
e. sudden
f. unexpected
g. unsurprising

Write your own sentence using the word **ABRUPT**.

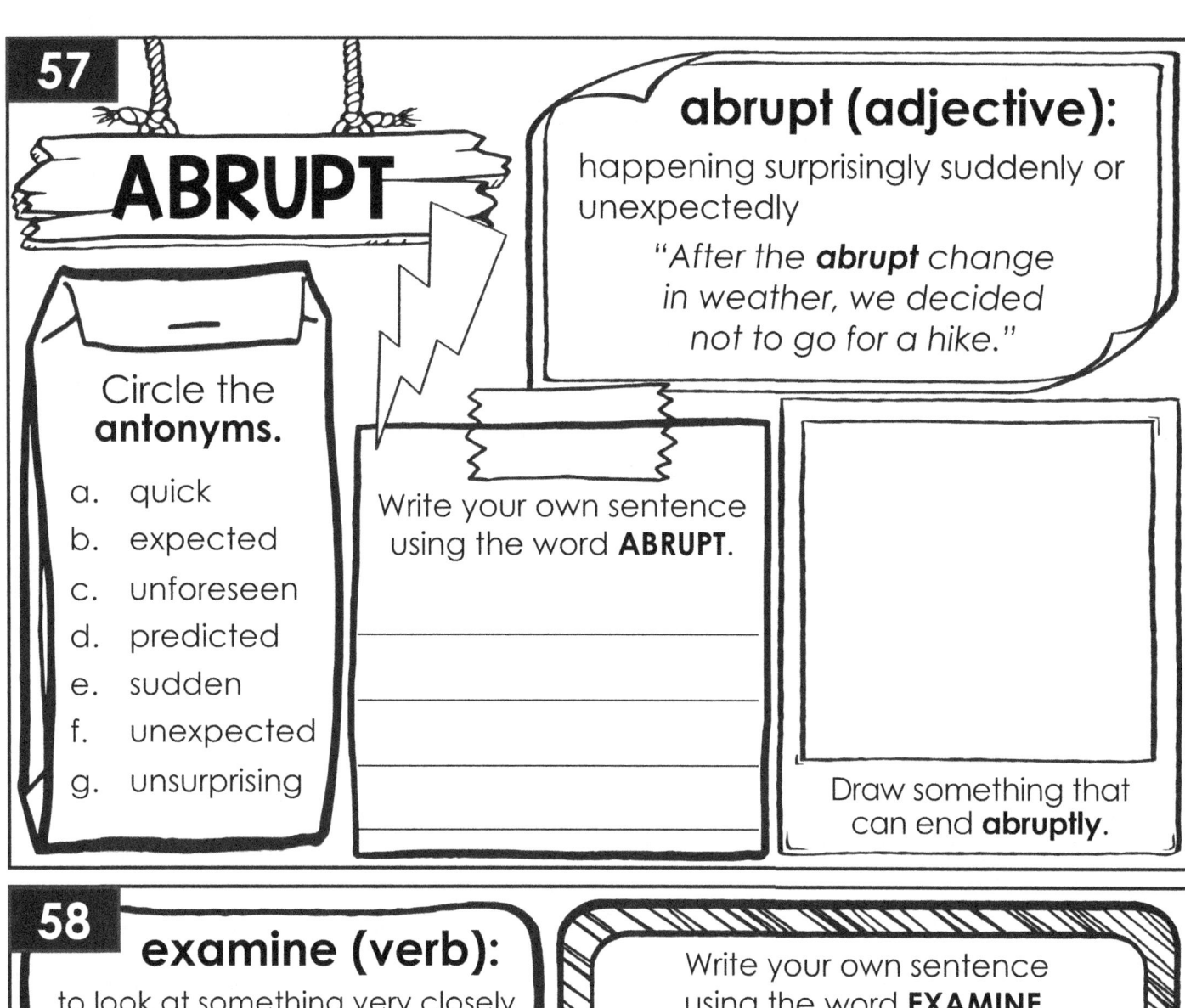

Draw something that can end **abruptly**.

58 EXAMINE

examine (verb): to look at something very closely and carefully; to investigate thoroughly

"The eye doctor will **examine** your eyes and vision for overall eye health."

Write your own sentence using the word **EXAMINE**.

Draw a picture of something you might **examine** through a microscope.

Circle the **synonyms.**

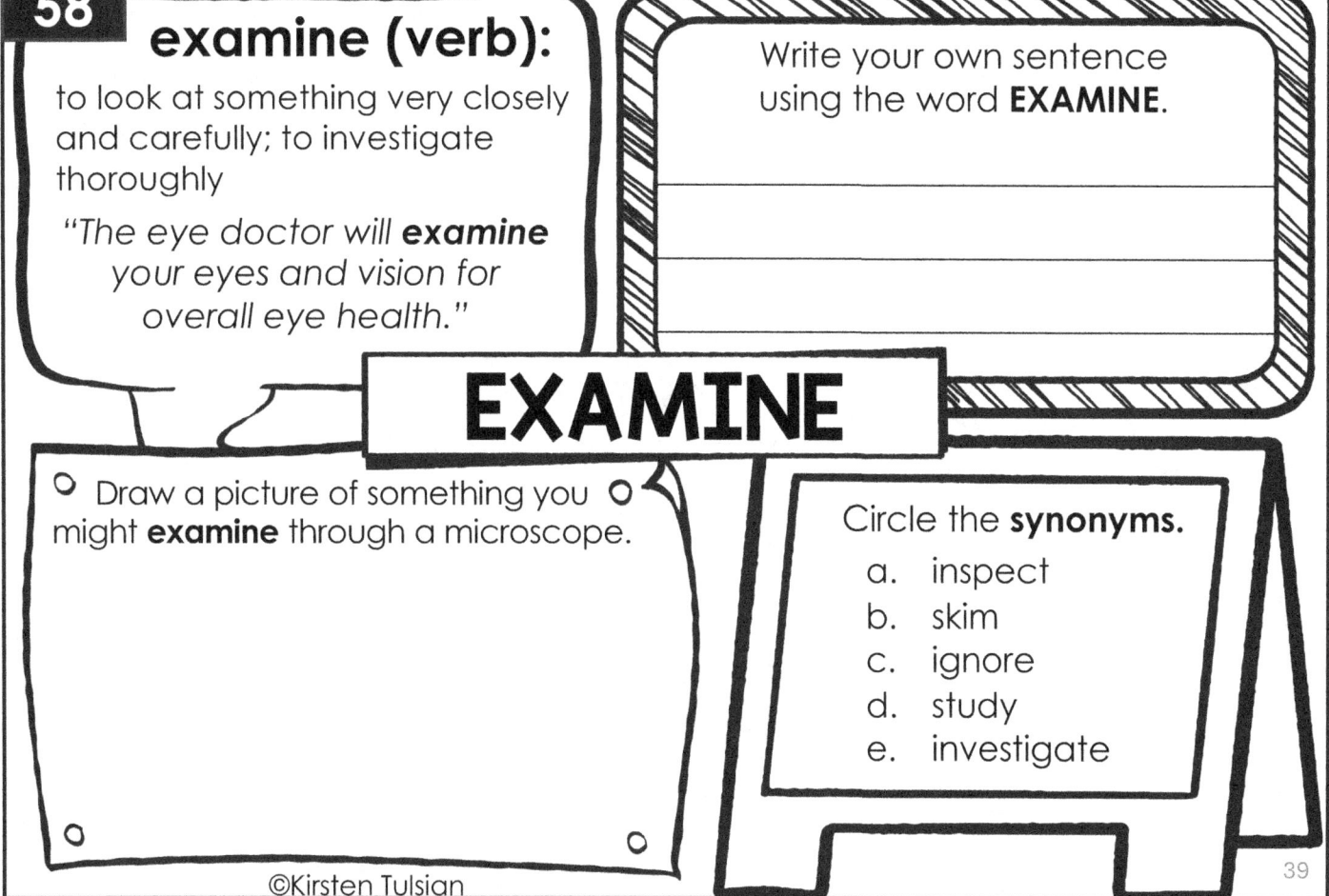

a. inspect
b. skim
c. ignore
d. study
e. investigate

59

banter (verb):
playful, friendly, and light-hearted teasing or joking

"The performers bantered with the audience at the end of the show."

Draw a picture of someone or something who **banters** with you.

BANTER

Write your own sentence using the word **BANTER**.

Circle the **synonyms**.
a. working
b. teasing
c. struggling
d. joking
e. kidding
f. fighting

60

subtle (adjective):
not obvious or easy to notice; faint or indirect.

"There was a subtle difference in his mood after he got off the phone."

Choose the best word to replace **SUBTLE** in the sentence below.

The color differences are **subtle**, but the first photo is more vibrant.
a. slight   c. uncomfortable
b. bright   d. noticeable

SUBTLE

Circle the **synonyms**.
a. loud
b. faint
c. obvious
d. clear
e. understated

Write your own sentence using the word **SUBTLE**.

©Kirsten Tulsian

61

duplicate (verb):
to make an exact copy of something; to do something in the same way

*"Just in case something happens, it's a great idea to **duplicate** and save a backup of your science report."*

DOODLE IT!

DUPLICATE

Write your own sentence using the word **DUPLICATE**.

Choose the best word to replace **DUPLICATE** in the sentence below.

It's hard to **duplicate** a flaky pie crust without using butter.

- a. mistake
- b. reproduce
- c. read
- d. protect

62

unbelievable (adjective):
so surprising or unlikely that it's hard to believe it's true

*"There are an **unbelievable** number of hummingbirds at our feeders this year!"*

Choose the best word to replace **UNBELIEVABLE** in the sentence below.

The amount of snow that fell overnight was **unbelievable**!

- a. average
- b. annoying
- c. disappointing
- d. incredible

UNBELIEVABLE

DOODLE IT!

Write your own sentence using the word **UNBELIEVABLE**.

63

distraught (adjective):
deeply upset, agitated, frantic, or worried;

*"Pedro was **distraught** when he got home and realized his dog had escaped from the backyard."*

Circle the **synonyms**.
a. content
b. frightened
c. terrified
d. frantic
e. peaceful
f. excited

DISTRAUGHT

Write your own sentence using the word **DISTRAUGHT**.

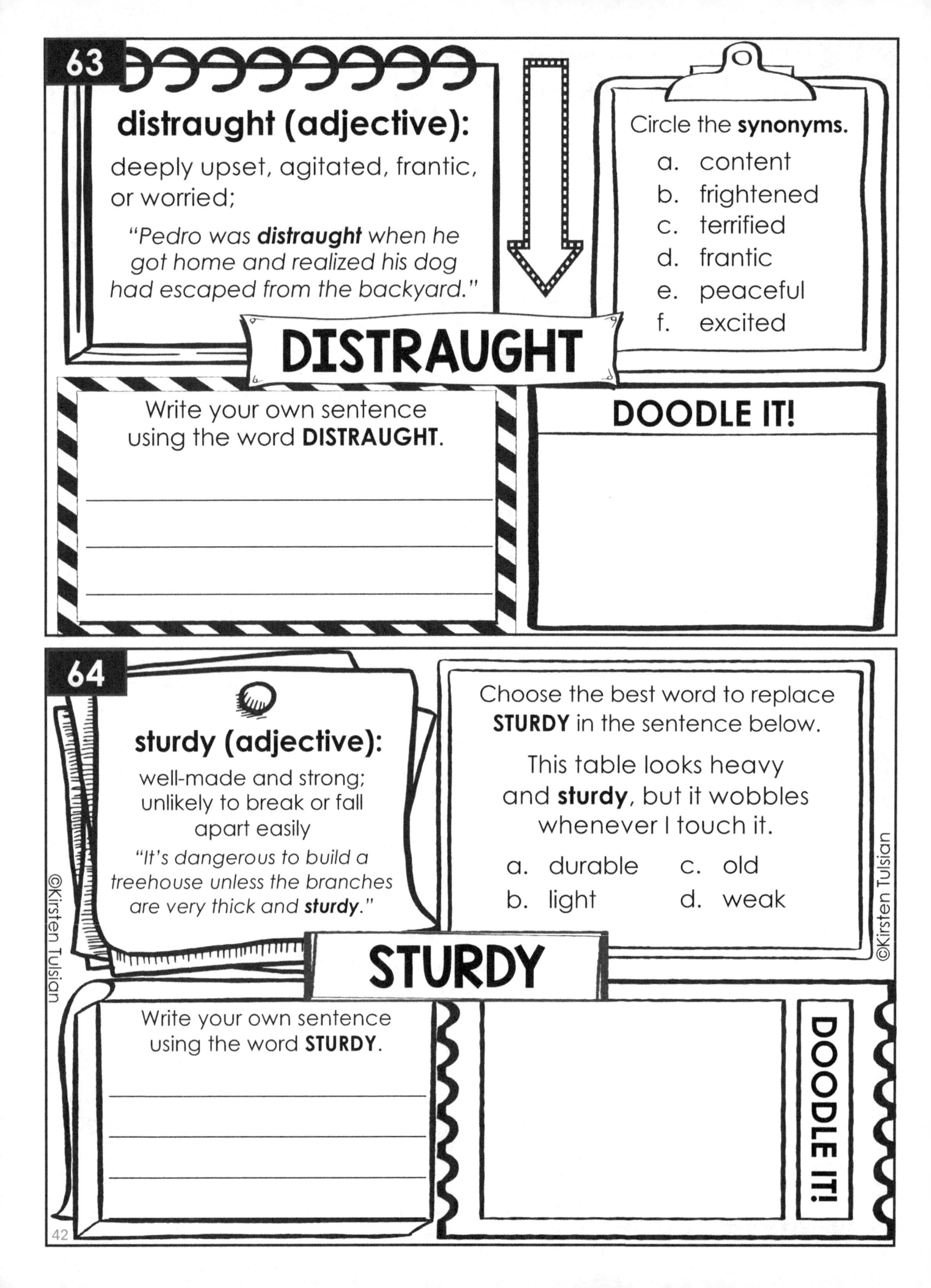

DOODLE IT!

64

sturdy (adjective):
well-made and strong; unlikely to break or fall apart easily

*"It's dangerous to build a treehouse unless the branches are very thick and **sturdy**."*

Choose the best word to replace **STURDY** in the sentence below.

This table looks heavy and **sturdy**, but it wobbles whenever I touch it.

a. durable   c. old
b. light   d. weak

STURDY

Write your own sentence using the word **STURDY**.

DOODLE IT!

65

DETECT

detect (verb):
to notice or discover something that might be hidden or not easily seen

*"This type of health condition is hard to **detect** in its early stages."*

Circle the **synonyms.**
a. lose
b. hide
c. find
d. locate
e. ignore
f. discover
g. recognize

Write your own sentence using the word **DETECT**.

DOODLE IT!

66

vibrant (adjective):
full of life, energy, enthusiasm, or bright color

*"Julia's **vibrant** personality brought so much joy and excitement to the party."*

Write your own sentence using the word **VIBRANT**.

VIBRANT

Draw a picture of a **vibrant** sunset.

Circle the **antonyms.**
a. lively
b. dull
c. energetic
d. uninteresting
e. lifeless

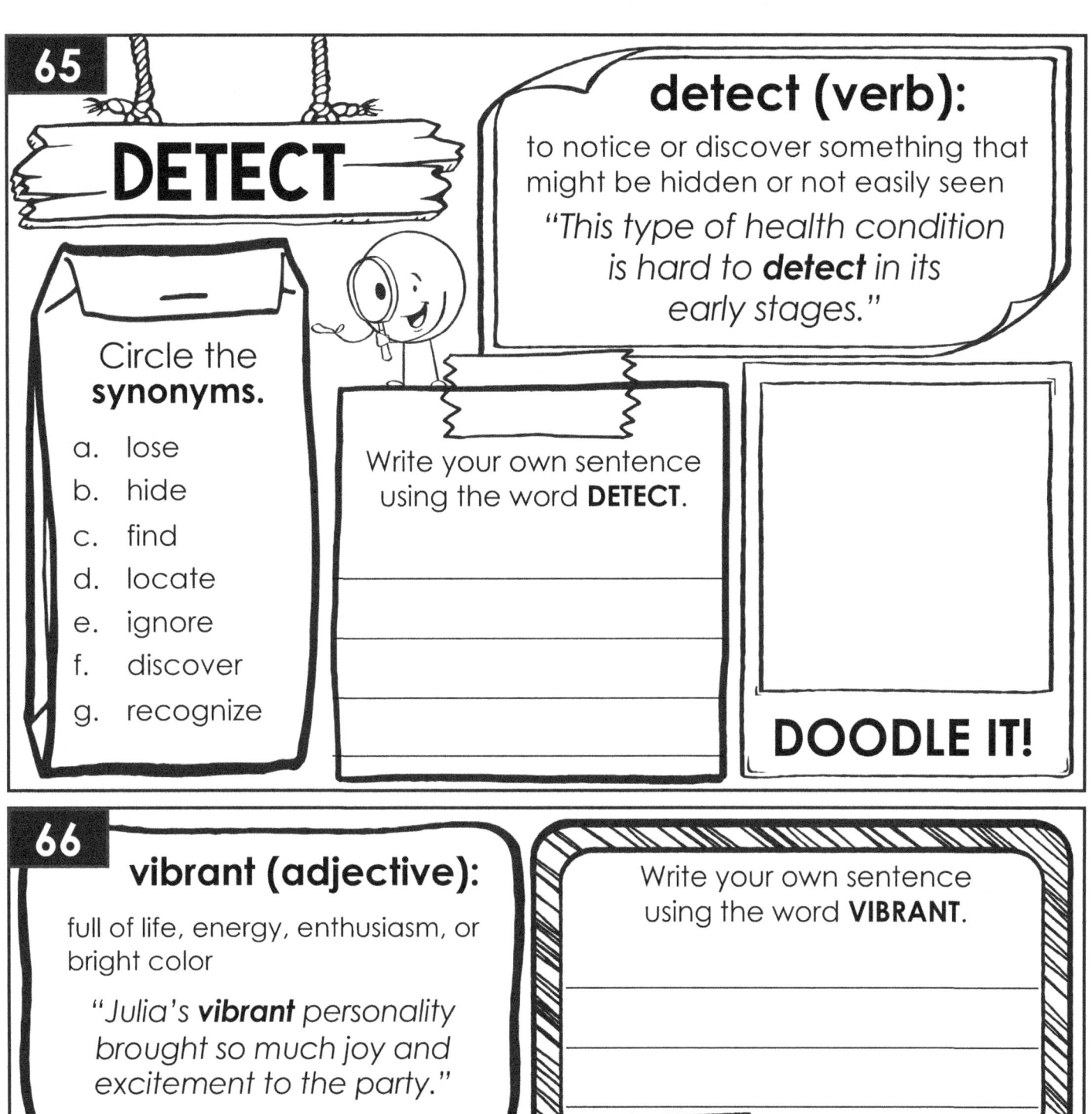

©Kirsten Tulsian

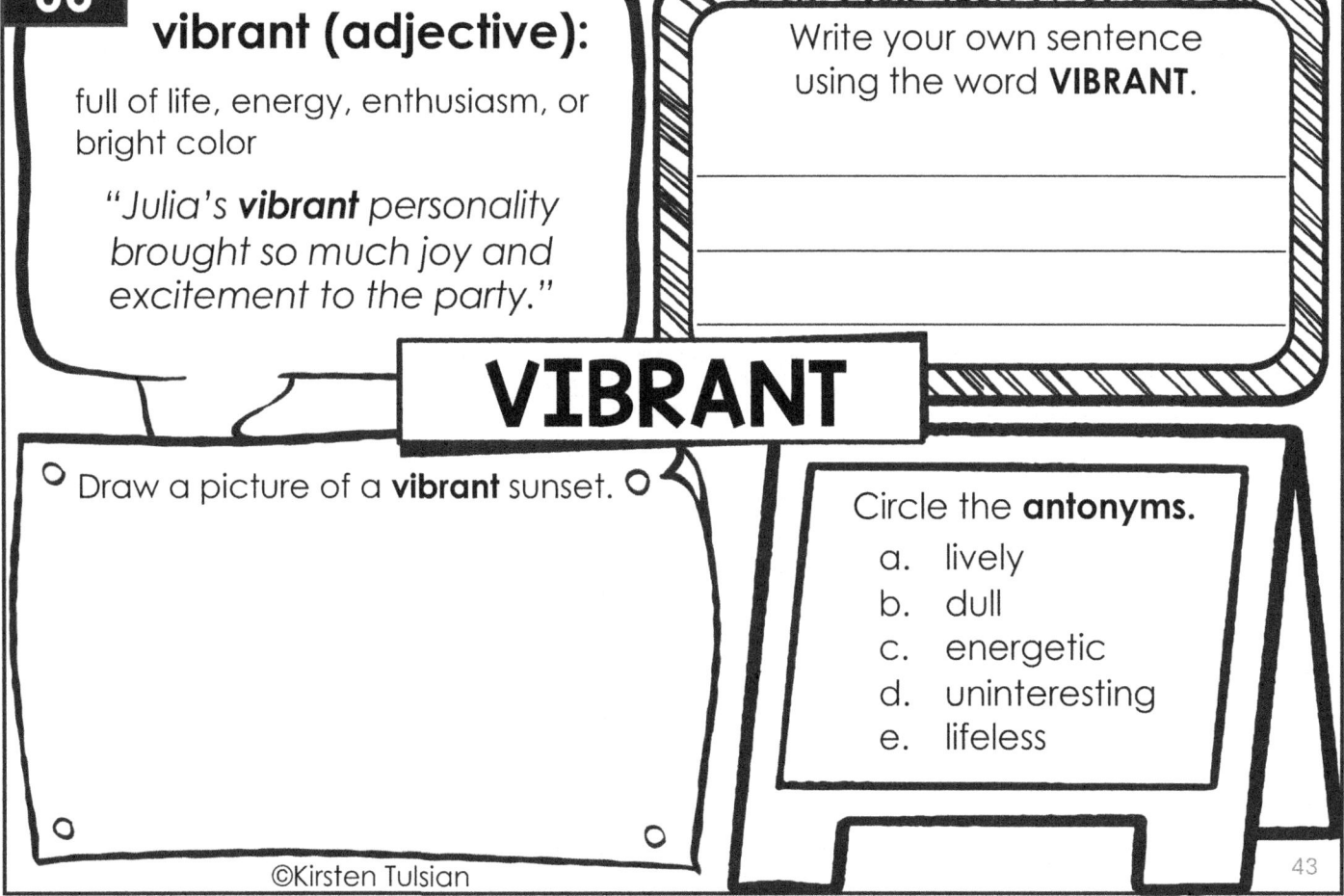

43

67

triumph (noun):
a great victory or achievement; a big win or success

*"There was a great feeling of **triumph** when our group finished the project."*

TRIUMPH

Draw a picture of a time when you experienced great success.

Write your own sentence using the word **TRIUMPH**.

Circle the **synonyms**.
a. victory
b. failure
c. achievement
d. accomplishment
e. success
f. disaster

68

fascinate (verb):
to make someone very interested or captivated by something

*"Bird-watching might be boring to you, but it **fascinates** me!"*

FASCINATE

Choose the best word to replace FASCINATE in the sentence below.
I will **fascinate** you with all my astronomy knowledge!
a. worry   c. annoy
b. captivate d. disgust

Write your own sentence using the word **FASCINATE**.

Fascinate an audience with your favorite doodle or drawing.

65 DETECT

detect (verb): to notice or discover something that might be hidden or not easily seen

*"This type of health condition is hard to **detect** in its early stages."*

Circle the **synonyms.**
a. lose
b. hide
c. find
d. locate
e. ignore
f. discover
g. recognize

Write your own sentence using the word **DETECT**.

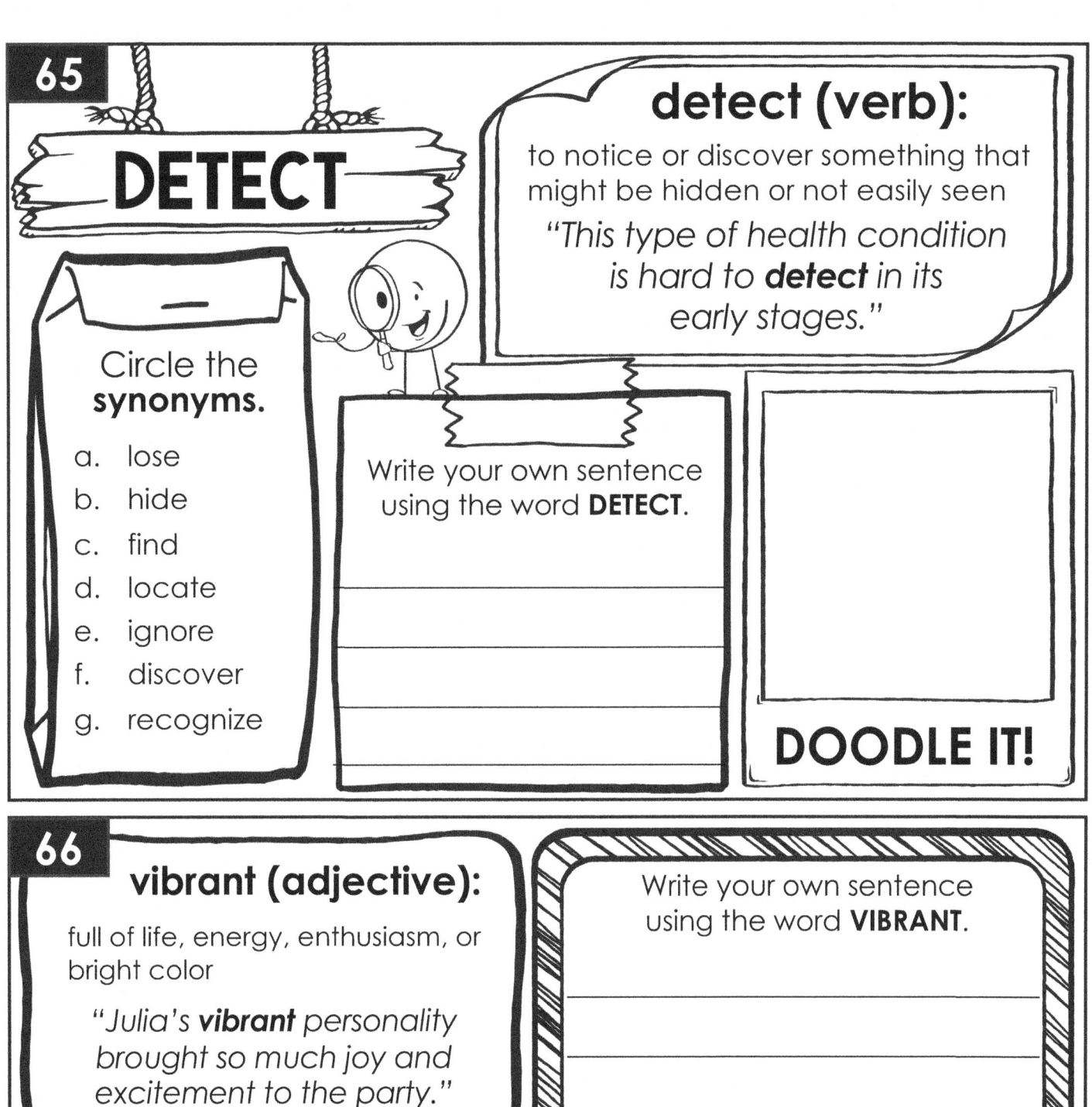

DOODLE IT!

66 VIBRANT

vibrant (adjective): full of life, energy, enthusiasm, or bright color

*"Julia's **vibrant** personality brought so much joy and excitement to the party."*

Write your own sentence using the word **VIBRANT**.

Draw a picture of a **vibrant** sunset.

Circle the **antonyms.**
a. lively
b. dull
c. energetic
d. uninteresting
e. lifeless

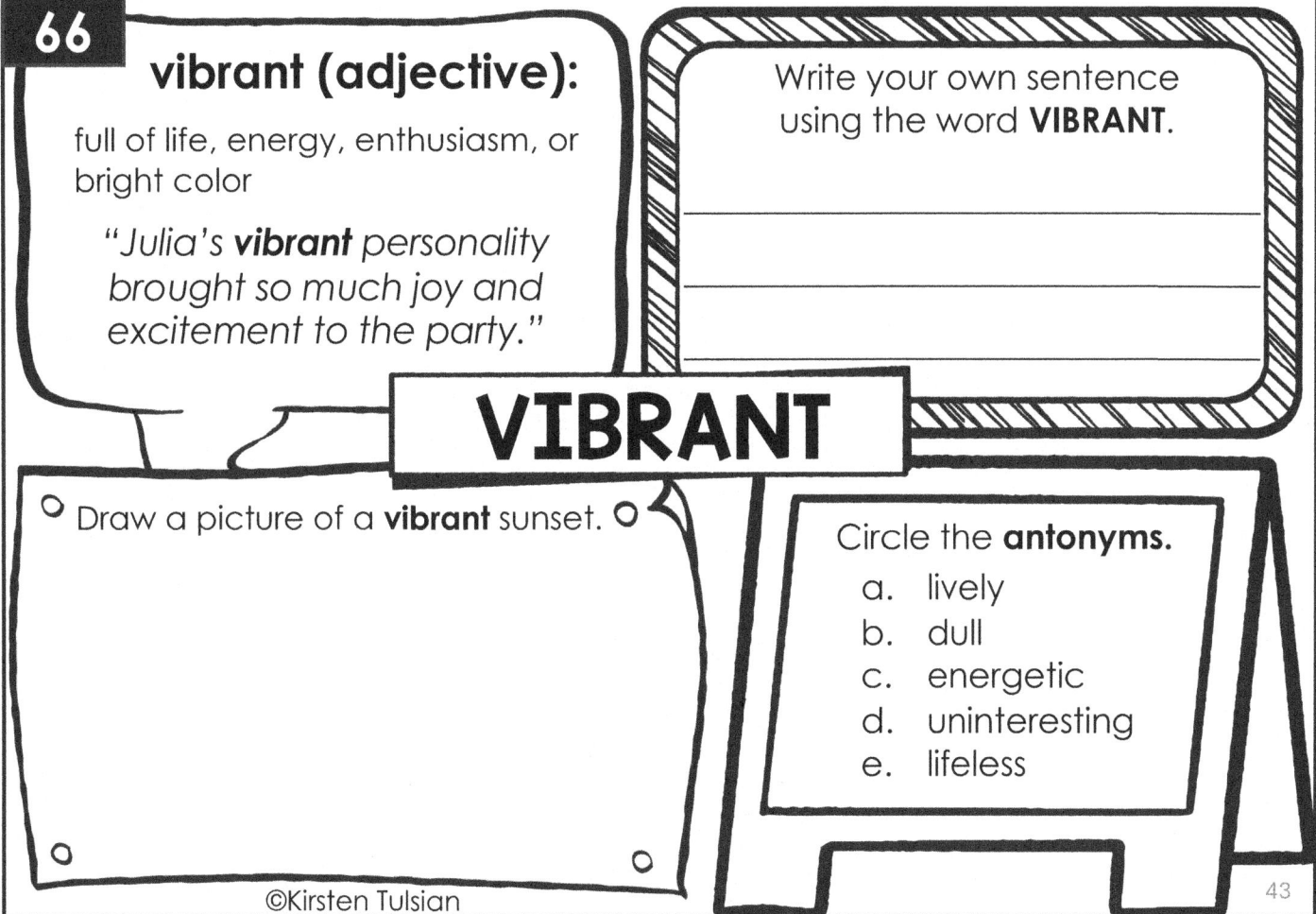

67

triumph (noun): a great victory or achievement; a big win or success

*"There was a great feeling of **triumph** when our group finished the project."*

Draw a picture of a time when you experienced great success.

TRIUMPH

Write your own sentence using the word **TRIUMPH**.

Circle the **synonyms.**
a. victory
b. failure
c. achievement
d. accomplishment
e. success
f. disaster

68

fascinate (verb): to make someone very interested or captivated by something

*"Bird-watching might be boring to you, but it **fascinates** me!"*

Choose the best word to replace **FASCINATE** in the sentence below.

I will **fascinate** you with all my astronomy knowledge!
a. worry
b. captivate
c. annoy
d. disgust

FASCINATE

Write your own sentence using the word **FASCINATE**.

Fascinate an audience with your favorite doodle or drawing.

©Kirsten Tulsian

69 navigate (verb):

to find one's way; to find the correct path, destination, or goal

*"My teacher helped me **navigate** a difficult situation with a classmate who was bullying me."*

Draw a picture of someone who helps you **navigate** life.

NAVIGATE

Write your own sentence using the word **NAVIGATE**.

Choose the best word to replace **NAVIGATE** in the sentence below.

The detailed map will **navigate** you in the right direction.

- a. mislead
- b. steer
- c. place
- d. forget

70 ordeal (noun):

a tough, challenging, difficult, or unpleasant experience

*"Crossing the bridge during the snowstorm was an **ordeal**."*

Choose the best word to replace **ORDEAL** in the sentence below.

It must have been quite an **ordeal** the fix the leaky faucet.

- a. comfort
- b. pleasure
- c. difficulty
- d. joy

DOODLE IT!

ORDEAL

Write your own sentence using the word **ORDEAL**.

©Kirsten Tulsian

71

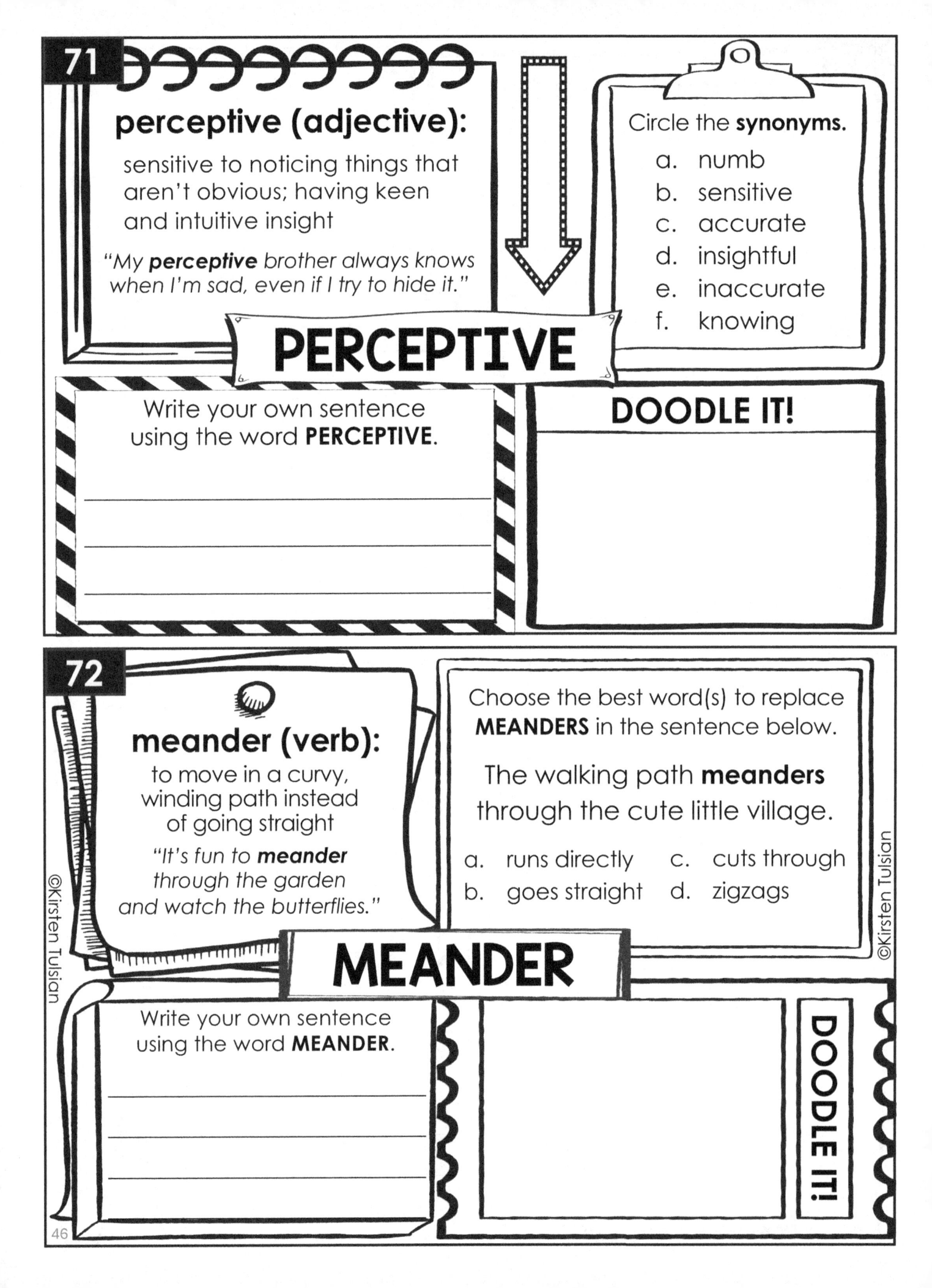

perceptive (adjective): sensitive to noticing things that aren't obvious; having keen and intuitive insight

*"My **perceptive** brother always knows when I'm sad, even if I try to hide it."*

Circle the **synonyms**.
a. numb
b. sensitive
c. accurate
d. insightful
e. inaccurate
f. knowing

PERCEPTIVE

Write your own sentence using the word **PERCEPTIVE**.

DOODLE IT!

72

meander (verb): to move in a curvy, winding path instead of going straight

*"It's fun to **meander** through the garden and watch the butterflies."*

Choose the best word(s) to replace **MEANDERS** in the sentence below.

The walking path **meanders** through the cute little village.

a. runs directly   c. cuts through
b. goes straight   d. zigzags

MEANDER

Write your own sentence using the word **MEANDER**.

DOODLE IT!

73 RECITE

recite (verb): to repeat something out loud from memory, usually in front of an audience

*"Lois can **recite** all the names of the states in the United States in alphabetical order."*

Circle the **synonyms.**
a. tell
b. listen
c. hush
d. report
e. rehearse
f. disturb
g. repeat

Write your own sentence using the word **RECITE**.

DOODLE IT!

74 OBVIOUS

obvious (adjective): easily seen or understood; easily perceived or apparent

*"Based on the empty food bowl, it was **obvious** that Spot was very hungry."*

Write your own sentence using the word **OBVIOUS**.

What is **obvious** about your personality when new people meet you? List three things.
1.
2.
3.

Circle the **antonyms.**
a. clear
b. hidden
c. noticeable
d. unclear
e. invisible

©Kirsten Tulsian

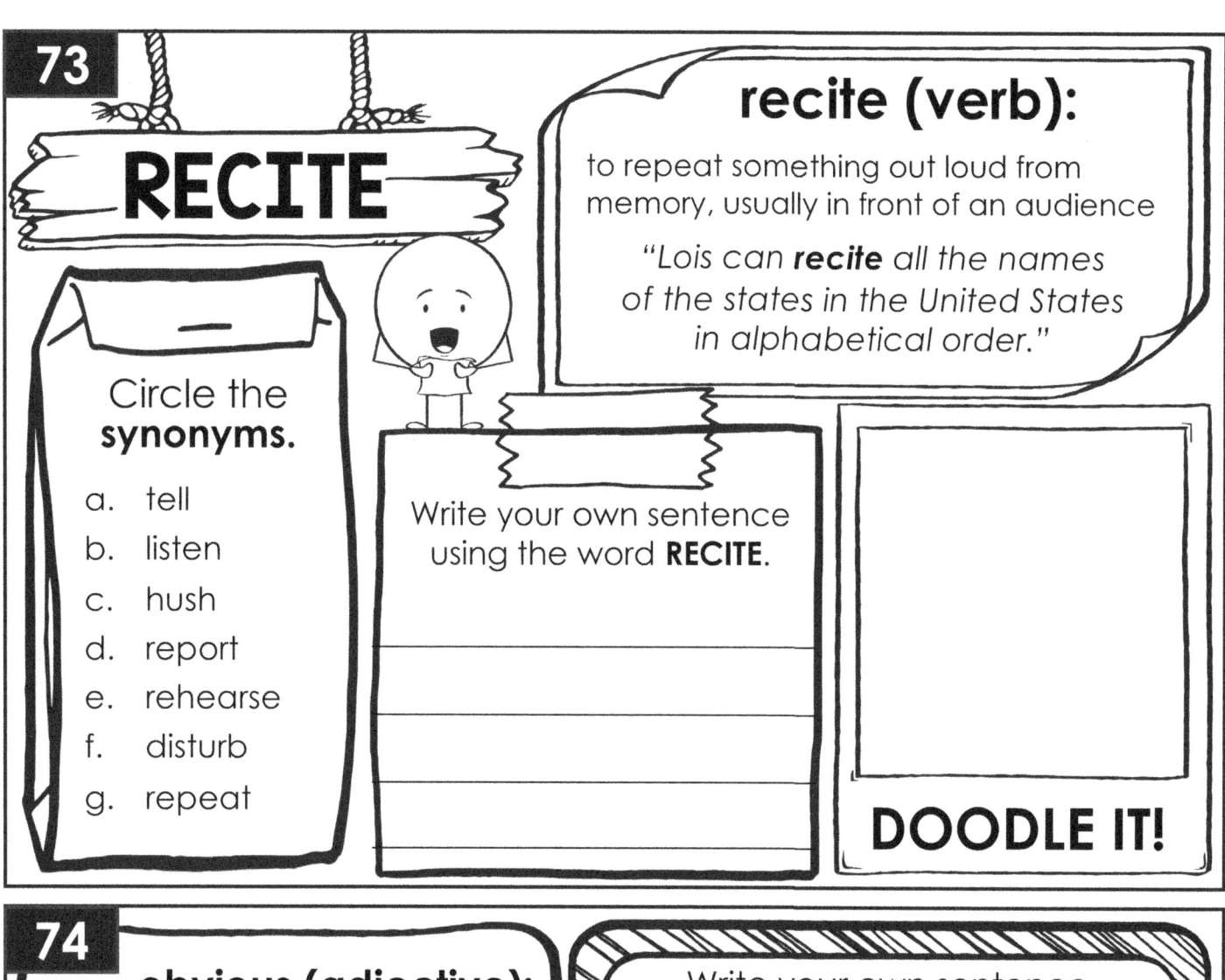

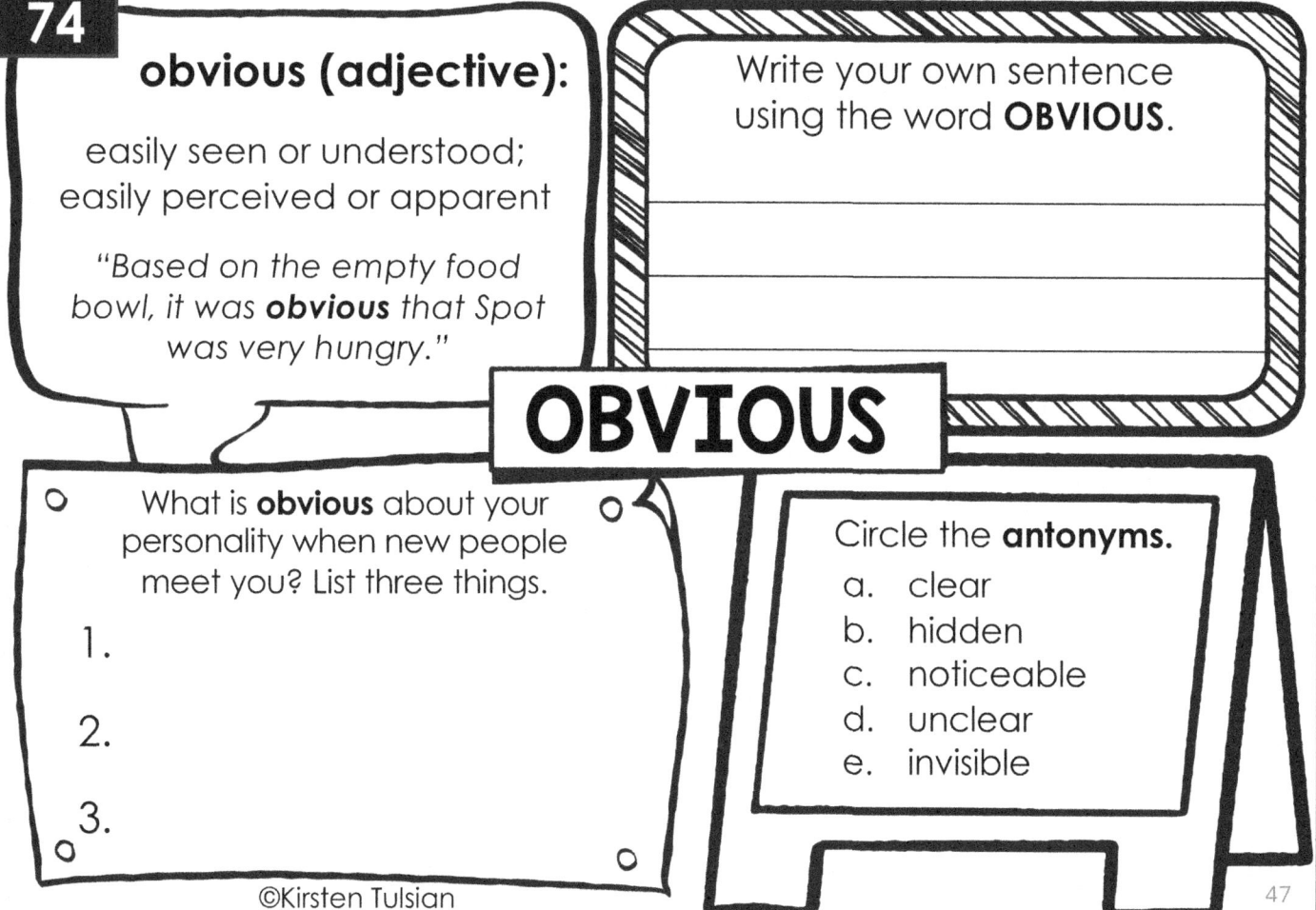

75

exclude (verb):
to leave someone or something out; to prevent participation

*"When Barney **excluded** me from his birthday party, I felt sad."*

Draw a picture of a time when you got **excluded** from something.

EXCLUDE

Write your own sentence using the word **EXCLUDE**.

Circle the **synonyms**.
a. include
b. prevent
c. reject
d. welcome
e. ignore
f. accept

76

murky (adjective):
something dark, cloudy, and hard to see through

*"It is impossible to see through the **murky** waters of the pond."*

Choose the best word to replace **MURKY** in the sentence below.

The **murky** air is thick with smoke from the campfire.
a. clear   c. light
b. cloudy   d. bright

MURKY

Write your own sentence using the word **MURKY**.

DOODLE IT!

77

enhance (verb):

to make something better or more attractive; to improve the quality or value of something

"Adding a little extra salt can **enhance** the flavor of the pasta dish."

ENHANCE

DOODLE IT!

Write your own sentence using the word **ENHANCE**.

Circle the **synonyms**.
a. improve
b. better
c. weaken
d. enrich
e. neglect
f. ignore

78

scoff (verb):

to laugh at or mock in a mean way when you believe something is silly or ridiculous

"My sister **scoffed** when I told her I wanted to be an NBA player."

Choose the best word to replace **SCOFF** in the sentence below.

It's not unusual for teenagers to **scoff** when their parents ask them to do something.

a. smirk
b. listen
c. behave
d. respond

DOODLE IT!

SCOFF

Write your own sentence using the word **SCOFF**.

79

perplexed (adjective): completely confused and baffled; filled with uncertainty

"Many people are **perplexed** when they watch a magic show."

PERPLEXED

Circle the **synonyms.**
a. puzzled
b. baffled
c. sure
d. certain
e. confused
f. bewildered

Write your own sentence using the word **PERPLEXED**.

DOODLE IT!

80

hazardous (adjective): dangerous or risky, potentially causing harm or injury

"The smoke from the fire contains **hazardous** chemicals."

HAZARDOUS

Choose the best word to replace **HAZARDOUS** in the sentence below.

It is against the law to send **hazardous** materials in the mail.

a. protected   c. unsafe
b. harmless   d. secure

Write your own sentence using the word **HAZARDOUS**.

DOODLE IT!

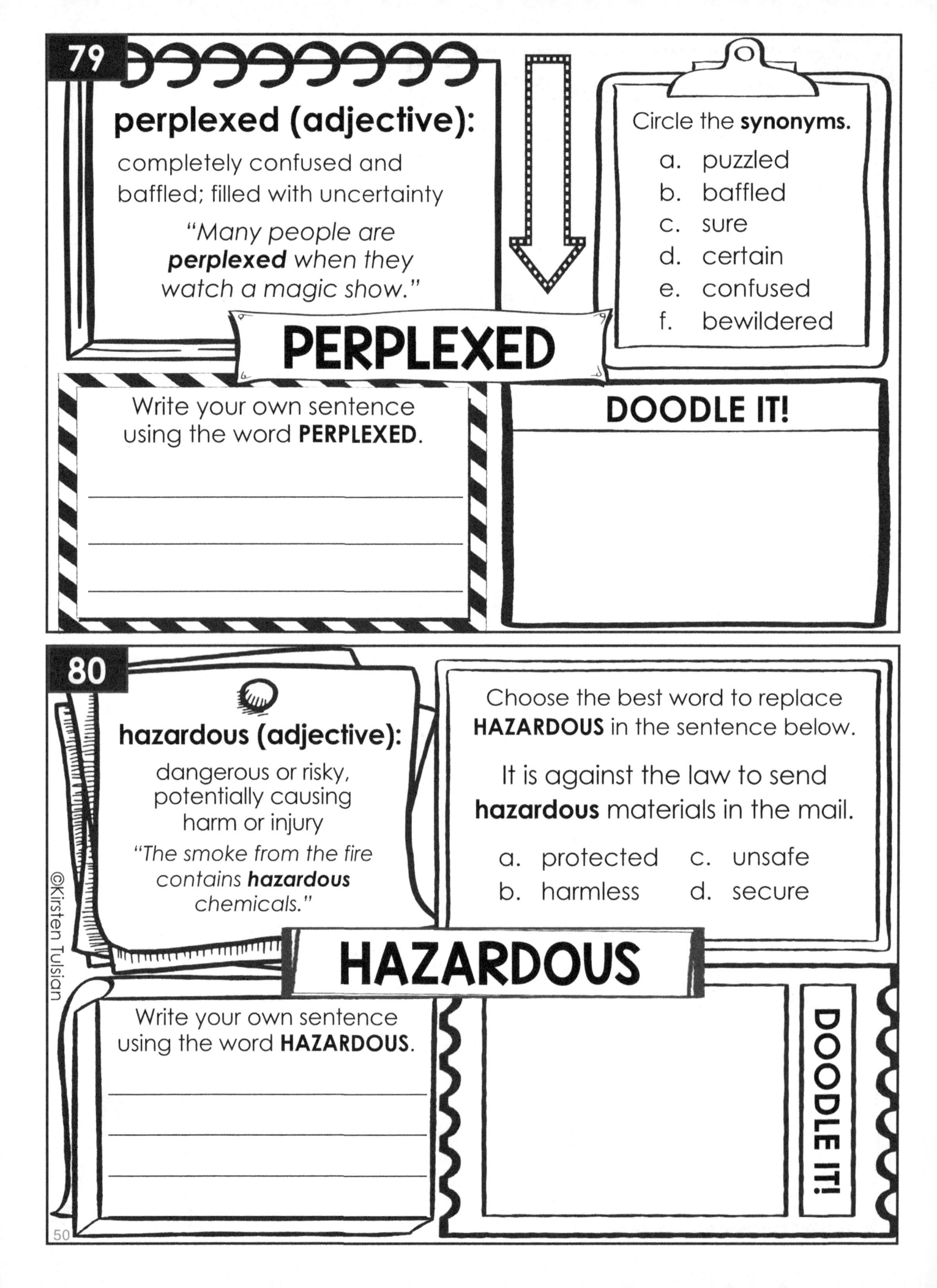

©Kirsten Tulsian

81 LURK

lurk (verb): to hide or sneak around, often waiting for the right moment to do something

"My aunt **lurked** behind the bushes, waiting to jump out and surprise me."

Circle the **synonyms**.
a. sneak
b. prowl
c. appear
d. hide
e. run
f. creep
g. leave

Write your own sentence using the word **LURK**.

DOODLE IT!

82 NOTEWORTHY

noteworthy (adjective): important, interesting, or special enough to pay attention to or remember

"His paintings are **noteworthy** for their beauty and attention to detail."

Write your own sentence using the word **NOTEWORTHY**.

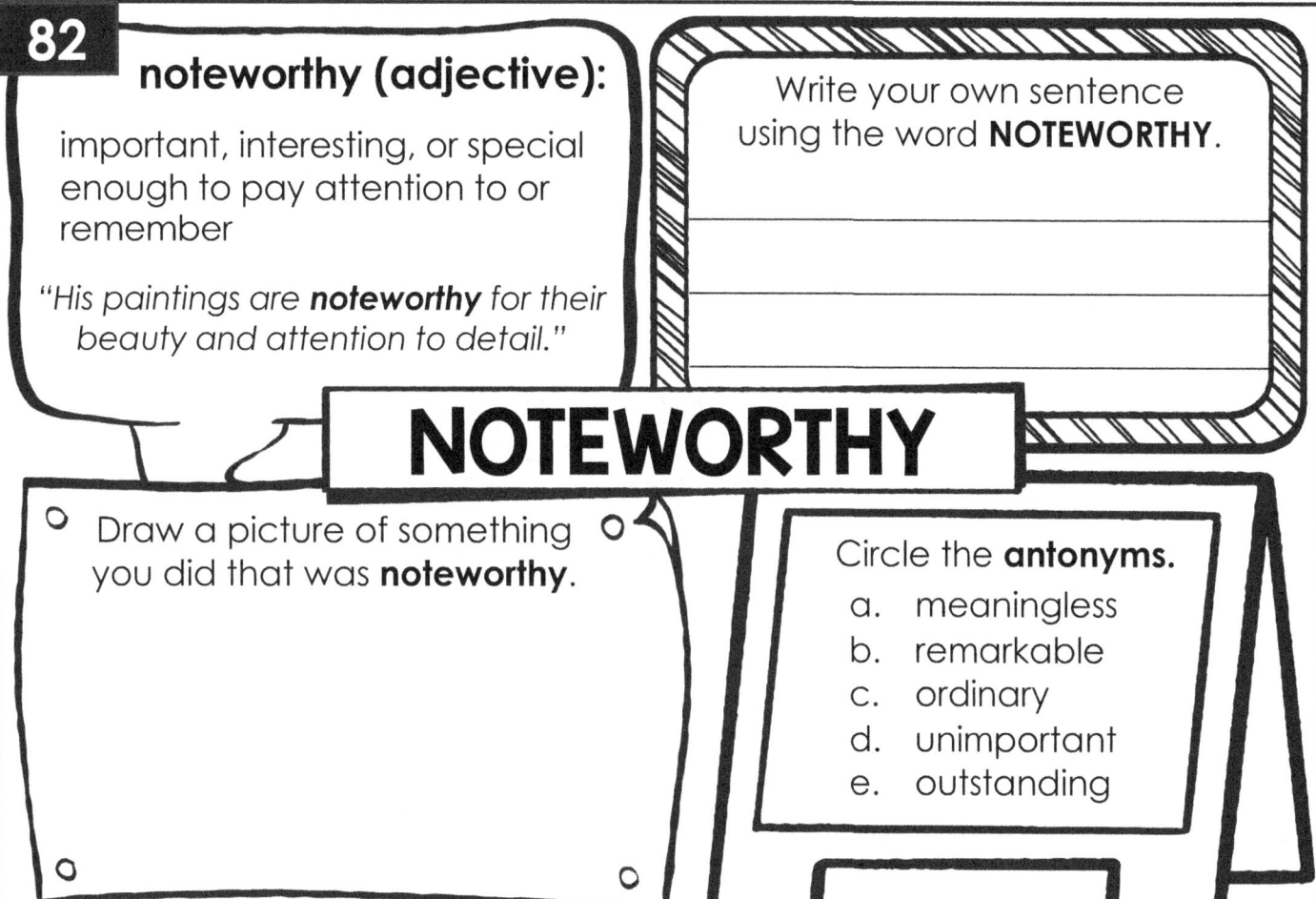

Draw a picture of something you did that was **noteworthy**.

Circle the **antonyms**.
a. meaningless
b. remarkable
c. ordinary
d. unimportant
e. outstanding

©Kirsten Tulsian

83

vivid (adjective):
bright, strong, and clear, like a cool picture or memory that feels real

"I had a **vivid** dream that I was flying through the city."

VIVID

Briefly describe a **vivid** dream you've had in the past.

Write your own sentence using the word **VIVID**.

Circle the **synonyms**.
a. lifelike
b. memorable
c. dull
d. realistic
e. boring
f. powerful

84

bewilder (verb):
to completely confuse, puzzle, or baffle

"My science test grade **bewildered** me because I thought I did well."

BEWILDER

Choose the best word to replace **BEWILDERED** in the sentence below.

Mrs. Jackson **bewilders** students with her complicated math problem.
a. calmed   c. baffled
b. soothed   d. pleased

Circle the **synonyms**.
a. perplex
b. satisfy
c. stun
d. surprise
e. comfort
f. cheer

Write your own sentence using the word **BEWILDER**.

DOODLE IT!

85

agile (adjective):
able to move quickly and easily; able to think quickly and cleverly

*"Cheetahs are one of the fastest and most **agile** animals in the world."*

AGILE

DOODLE IT!

Write your own sentence using the word **AGILE**.

Choose the best word to replace **AGILE** in the sentence below.

Sam is quick and **agile**, which helped us win the game.

a. lazy
b. stiff
c. weak
d. athletic

86

solitary (adjective):
being alone without others around; doing something by yourself

*"When Mina feels sad or angry, she takes a **solitary** walk in the park."*

Choose the best word to replace **SOLITARY** in the sentence below.

Dogs generally like to be social, while cats prefer a **solitary** life.

a. silly   c. reclusive
b. fun   d. held

SOLITARY

DOODLE IT!

Write your own sentence using the word **SOLITARY**.

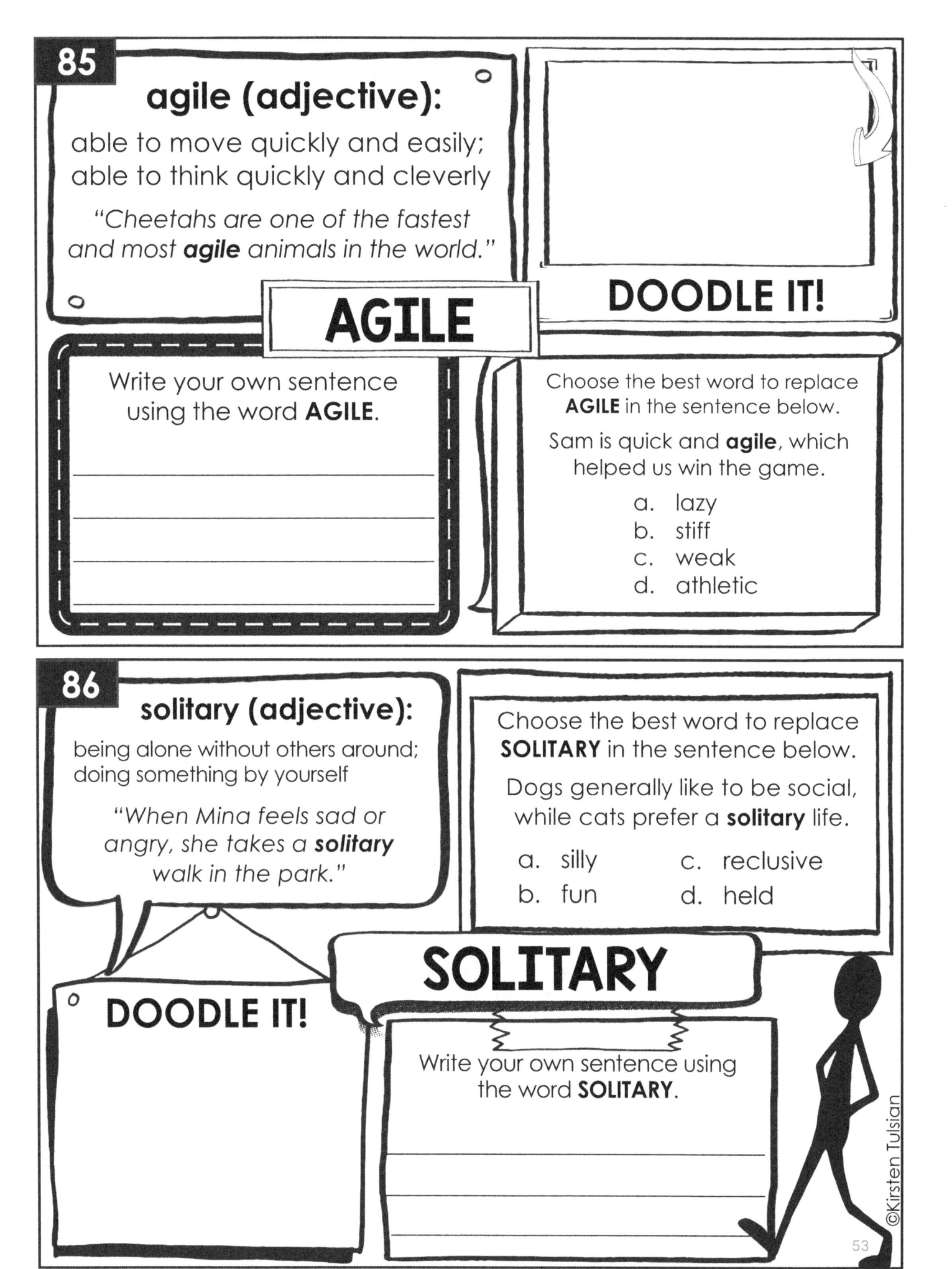

87

retrieve (verb):
to get or bring something back; to regain possession of

*"Can you please **retrieve** my house key from my backpack?"*

RETRIEVE

Circle the **synonyms**.
a. get
b. lose
c. bring
d. break
e. fetch
f. destroy

Write your own sentence using the word **RETRIEVE**.

DOODLE IT!

88

rubble (noun):
broken pieces of things, like bricks or rocks left behind after something is destroyed

*"The house crumbled into a pile of **rubble** after the earthquake."*

RUBBLE

Choose the best word to replace **RUBBLE** in the sentence below.

We found our dog's favorite toy under a pile of **rubble** in the backyard.

a. gems
b. leaves
c. debris
d. supplies

Write your own sentence using the word **RUBBLE**.

DOODLE IT!

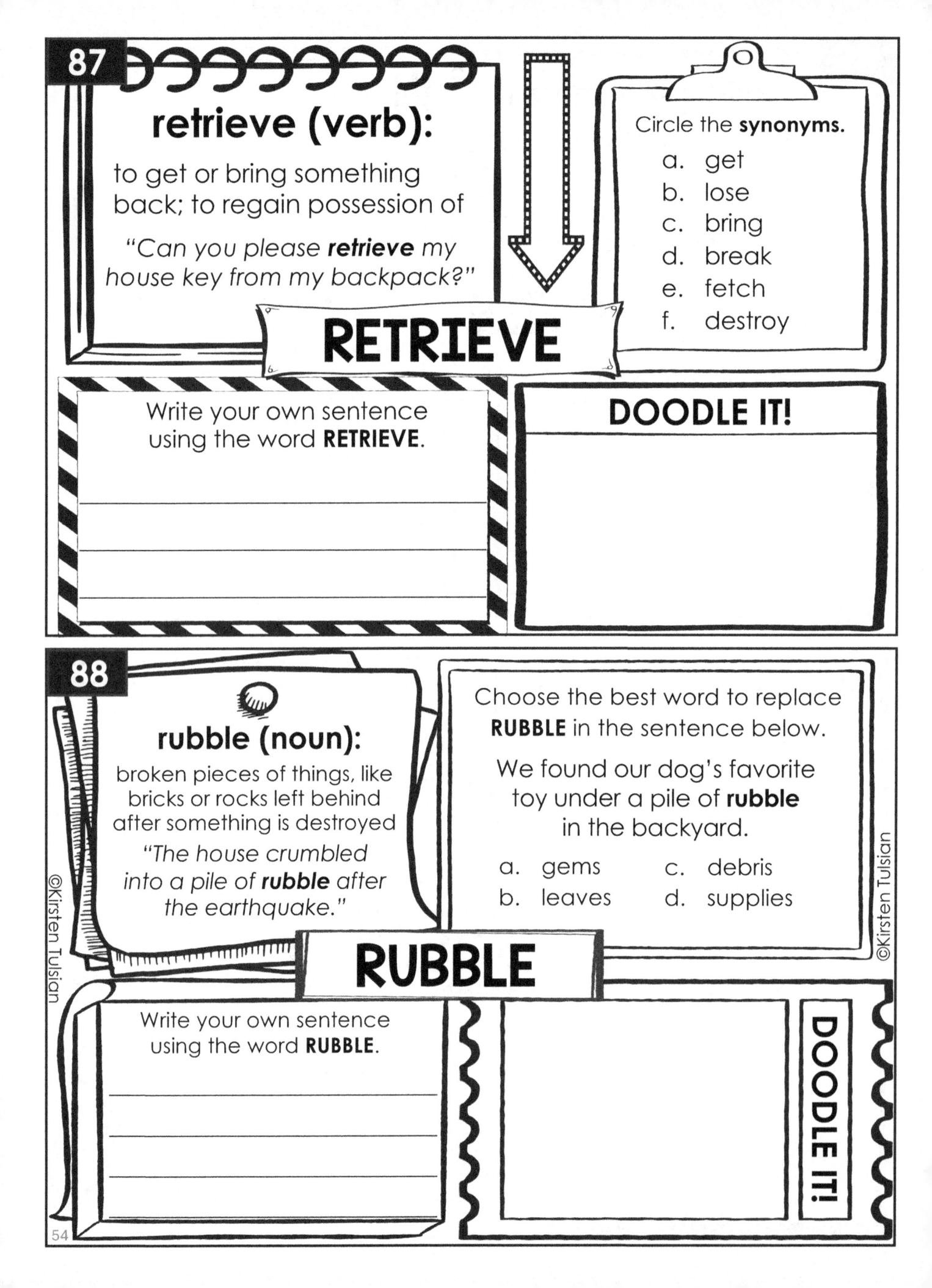

©Kirsten Tulsian

89 — LURE

lure (verb): to draw or attract; to tempt one to do something or go somewhere

*"The delicious burritos **lure** me to the restaurant, The Red Iguana, every time I get to choose where we'll eat."*

Circle the **synonyms.**
a. tempt
b. disgust
c. lose
d. entice
e. persuade
f. warn
g. attract

Write your own sentence using the word **LURE**.

What **lures** you to your favorite restaurant? Draw it.

90 — VISIBLE

visible (adjective): able to be seen; observable

*"On a clear night, the moon is **visible** through the trees in my front yard."*

Write your own sentence using the word **VISIBLE**.

Draw a picture of something that is **visible** from the front of your home.

Circle the **antonyms.**
a. hidden
b. noticeable
c. invisible
d. unclear
e. seeable

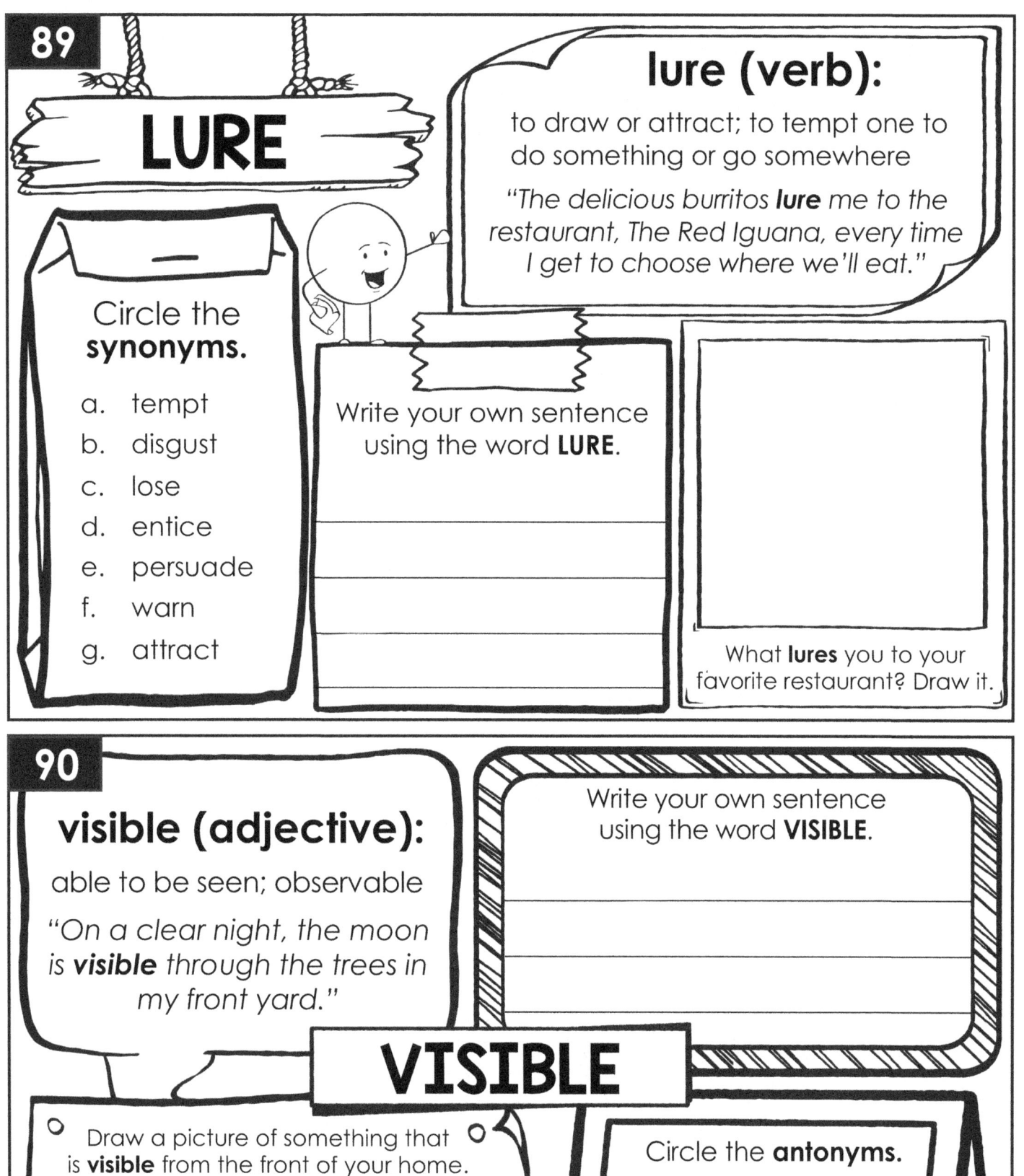

©Kirsten Tulsian

91. provoke (verb):

to make someone or something angry or upset on purpose or to cause a reaction or feeling

"Grabbing a dog's tail might **provoke** it to bite you."

Briefly describe a time when someone **provoked** you.

PROVOKE

Write your own sentence using the word **PROVOKE**.

Circle the **synonyms**.
a. inform
b. aggravate
c. teach
d. irritate
e. help
f. anger

92. discard (verb):

to throw away or get rid of

"After you finish eating your lunch, you can **discard** your trash in the garbage."

Choose the best word to replace DISCARD in the sentence below.

Discard your paper and plastic items in the recycling bin next to the trash.
a. Hold
b. Keep
c. Accept
d. Dump

DISCARD

Circle the **antonyms**.
a. reject
b. use
c. throw away
d. keep
e. trash
f. hold onto

Write your own sentence using the word **DISCARD**.

DOODLE IT!

©Kirsten Tulsian

93

reluctant (adjective):

not wanting to do something and being slow or hesitant to do it

*"I was **reluctant** the first time I tried an avocado, but I loved it!"*

Draw a picture of something you were **reluctant** to try.

RELUCTANT

Write your own sentence using the word **RELUCTANT**.

Circle the **synonyms.**
a. hesitant
b. unsure
c. excited
d. cautious
e. eager
f. enthusiastic

94

miniature (adjective):

very small, like a smaller version of something else, or a copy made on a small scale

*"When I was little, I had a **miniature** dollhouse with tiny people and furniture."*

Choose the best word to replace **MINIATURE** in the sentence below.

Aaron created a **miniature** version of a castle with modeling clay.

a. giant   c. normal
b. tiny   d. important

DOODLE IT!

MINIATURE

Write your own sentence using the word **MINIATURE**.

95

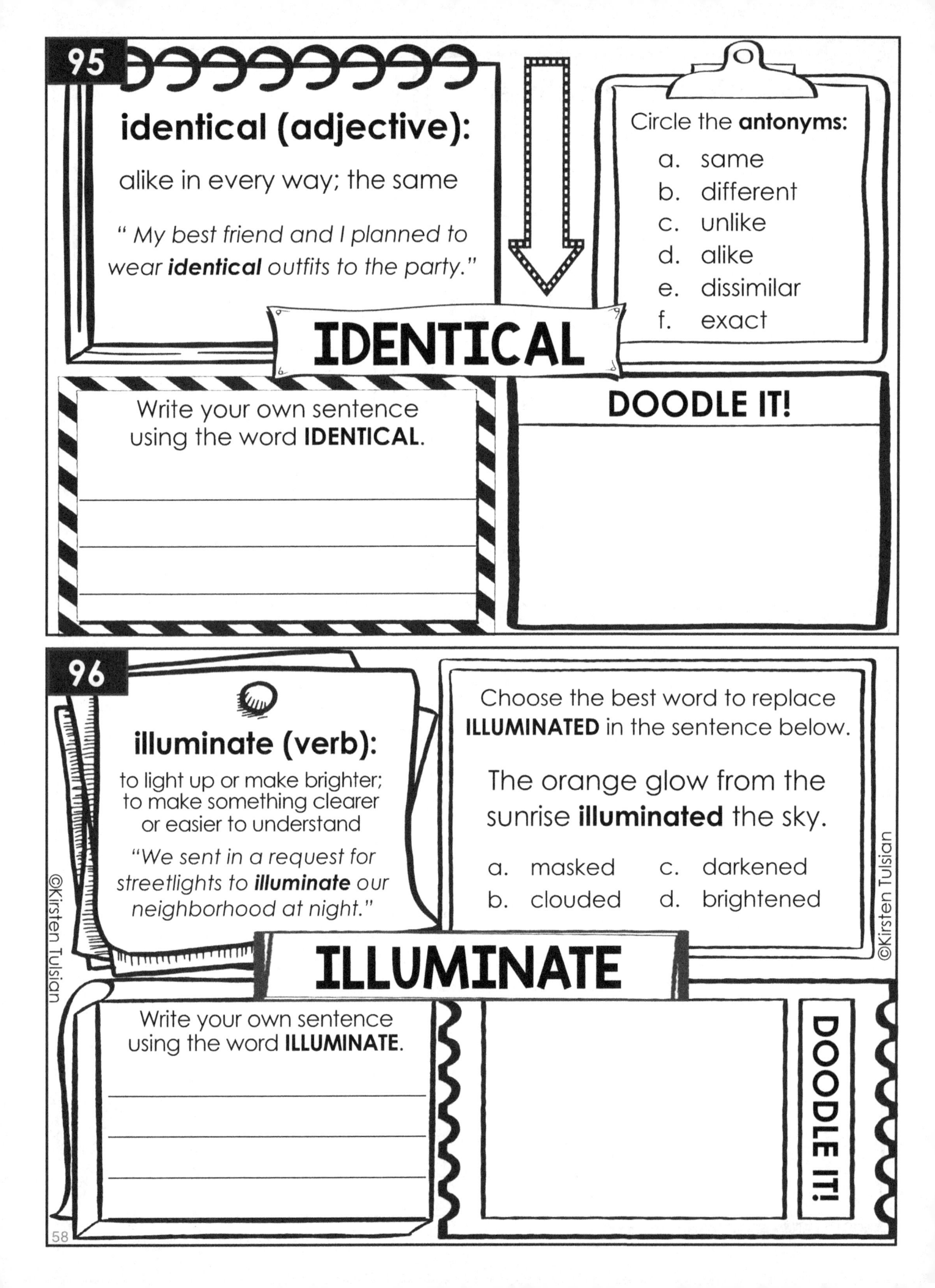

identical (adjective):

alike in every way; the same

"*My best friend and I planned to wear **identical** outfits to the party.*"

Circle the antonyms:
a. same
b. different
c. unlike
d. alike
e. dissimilar
f. exact

IDENTICAL

Write your own sentence using the word **IDENTICAL**.

DOODLE IT!

96

illuminate (verb):

to light up or make brighter; to make something clearer or easier to understand

"*We sent in a request for streetlights to **illuminate** our neighborhood at night.*"

Choose the best word to replace **ILLUMINATED** in the sentence below.

The orange glow from the sunrise **illuminated** the sky.

a. masked
b. clouded
c. darkened
d. brightened

ILLUMINATE

Write your own sentence using the word **ILLUMINATE**.

DOODLE IT!

97

IRATE

irate (adjective):
very angry; furious

*"My dad was **irate** when my older brother's friends toilet-papered our house."*

Circle the **antonyms.**

a. enraged
b. calm
c. furious
d. outraged
e. peaceful
f. livid
g. happy

Write your own sentence using the word **IRATE**.

DOODLE IT!

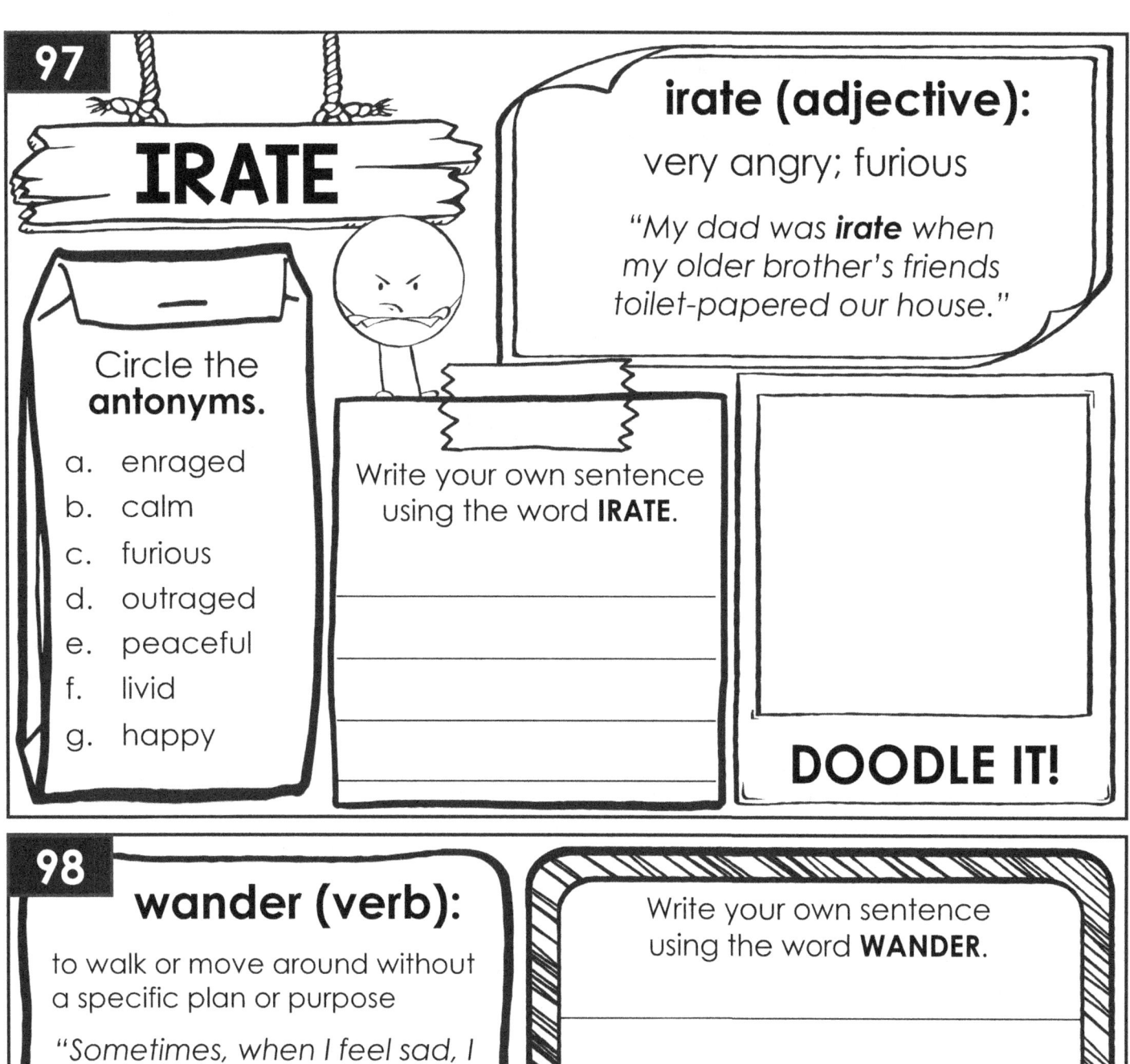

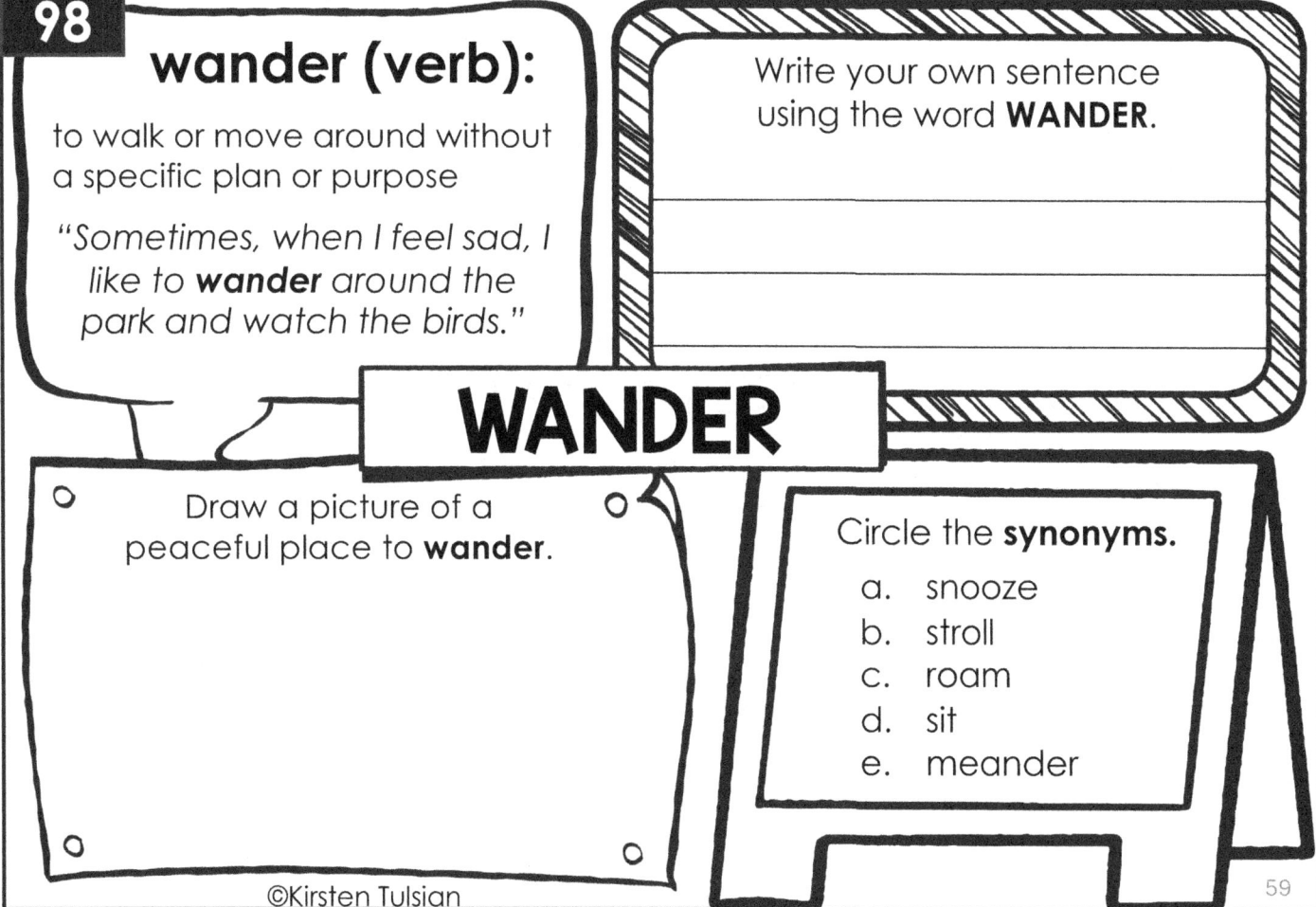

98

wander (verb):
to walk or move around without a specific plan or purpose

*"Sometimes, when I feel sad, I like to **wander** around the park and watch the birds."*

Write your own sentence using the word **WANDER**.

WANDER

Draw a picture of a peaceful place to **wander**.

Circle the **synonyms.**

a. snooze
b. stroll
c. roam
d. sit
e. meander

©Kirsten Tulsian

99

essential (adjective):
absolutely needed or necessary; extremely important

*"Fruits and vegetables are **essential** components of a balanced diet."*

Draw a picture of three **essential** items you need to live.

ESSENTIAL

Write your own sentence using the word **ESSENTIAL**.

Circle the **synonyms**.
a. vital
b. necessary
c. required
d. optional
e. needed
f. unnecessary

100

destructive (adjective):
causing great harm or damage

*"The storm was so **destructive** that it knocked down many trees and power lines."*

Choose the best word to replace **DESTRUCTIVE** in the sentence below.

Violent video games and movies can have a **destructive** impact on kids.
a. slight   c. positive
b. minimal   d. devastating

DESTRUCTIVE

Circle the **synonyms**.
a. creative
b. disastrous
c. negative
d. useful
e. damaging

Write your own sentence using the word **DESTRUCTIVE**.

©Kirsten Tulsian

101

exaggerate (verb):

to make something seem bigger, better, or worse than it really is

*"My sister always **exaggerates** when I ask her how much homework she has."*

EXAGGERATE

DOODLE IT!

Write your own sentence using the word **EXAGGERATE**.

Choose the best word(s) to replace **EXAGGERATES** in the sentence below.

He **exaggerates** when he talks about how far he walks to school.

- a. hides
- b. stretches the truth
- c. screams
- d. laughs

102

benefit (noun):

something good or helpful

*"One **benefit** of going to school early is getting extra help with homework."*

Choose the best word to replace **BENEFIT** in the sentence below.

A significant **benefit** of pet ownership is having a built-in best friend!

- a. hindrance
- b. misfortune
- c. disadvantage
- d. advantage

How do you **benefit** from getting an education? Draw a picture.

BENEFIT

Write your own sentence using the word **BENEFIT**.

©Kirsten Tulsian

103

swelter (verb):
to be uncomfortably hot; to sweat, suffer, or be faint from heat

*"Our air conditioning broke, and we were **sweltering** in the summer heat."*

SWELTER

Circle the **synonyms**.
a. shiver
b. sweat
c. scorch
d. freeze
e. bake
f. crack

Write your own sentence using the word **SWELTER**.

DOODLE IT!

104

dollop (noun):
a shapeless mass or blob of something, especially soft food

*"I like to add a **dollop** of whipped cream on top of my pumpkin pie."*

DOLLOP

Choose the best word to replace **DOLLOP** in the sentence below.

My mom placed a **dollop** of chocolate ice cream on each piece of cake.

a. bowl
b. glob
c. carton
d. gallon

Write your own sentence using the word **DOLLOP**.

DOODLE IT!

©Kirsten Tulsian

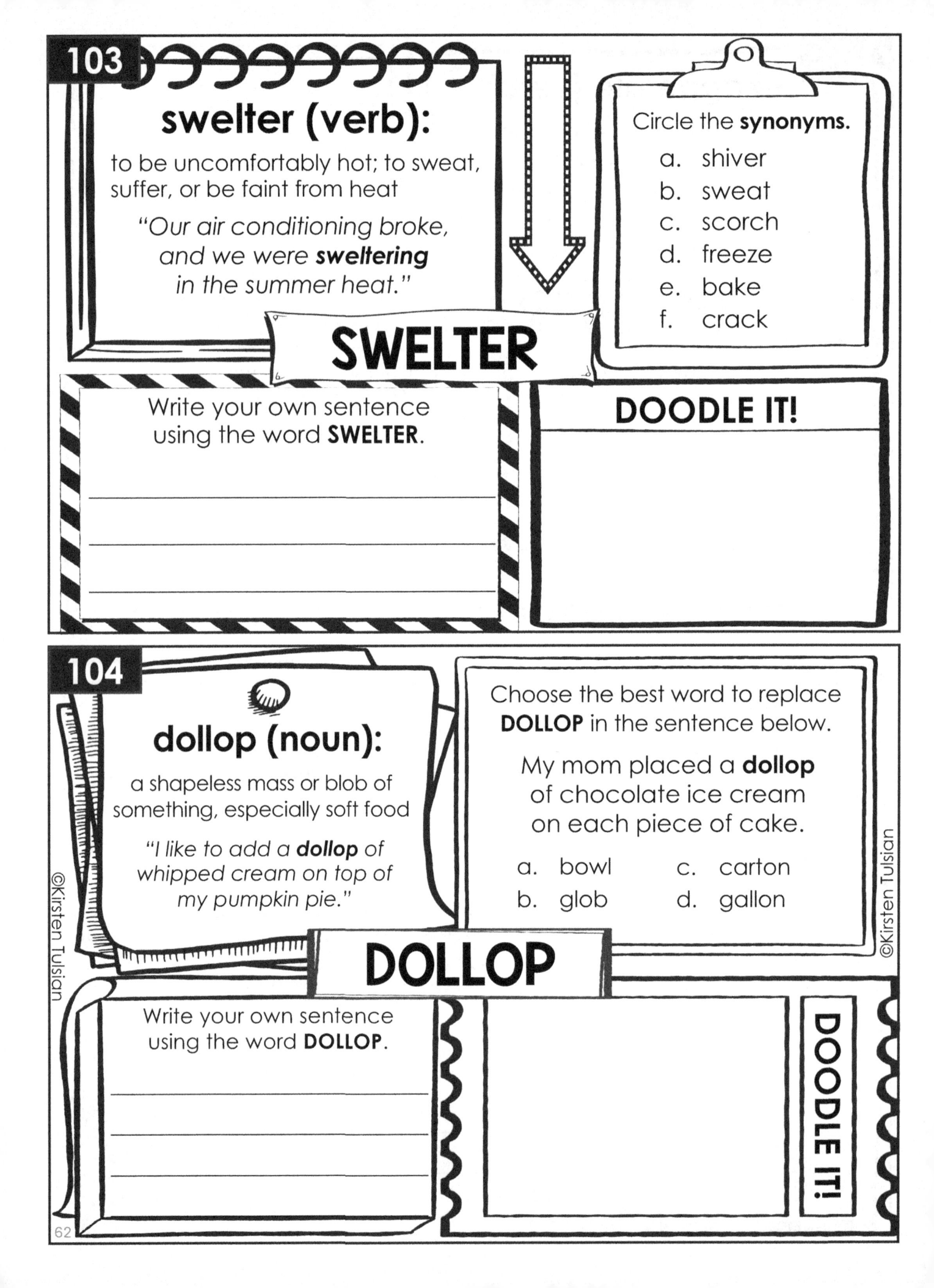

105 TIDY

tidy (adjective): arranged neatly and in order; organized and clean

*"It is important for me to keep my bedroom **tidy** at all times."*

Circle the **synonyms.**
a. clean
b. neat
c. messy
d. orderly
e. organized
f. uncluttered
g. sloppy

Write your own sentence using the word **TIDY**.

DOODLE IT!

106 EFFECTIVE

effective (adjective): working well and producing the desired result

*"Wearing a raincoat is an **effective** way to stay dry during thunderstorms."*

Write your own sentence using the word **EFFECTIVE**.

Draw a picture of one **effective** strategy for staying healthy.

Circle the **antonyms.**
a. useless
b. worthless
c. efficient
d. ineffective
e. useful

©Kirsten Tulsian

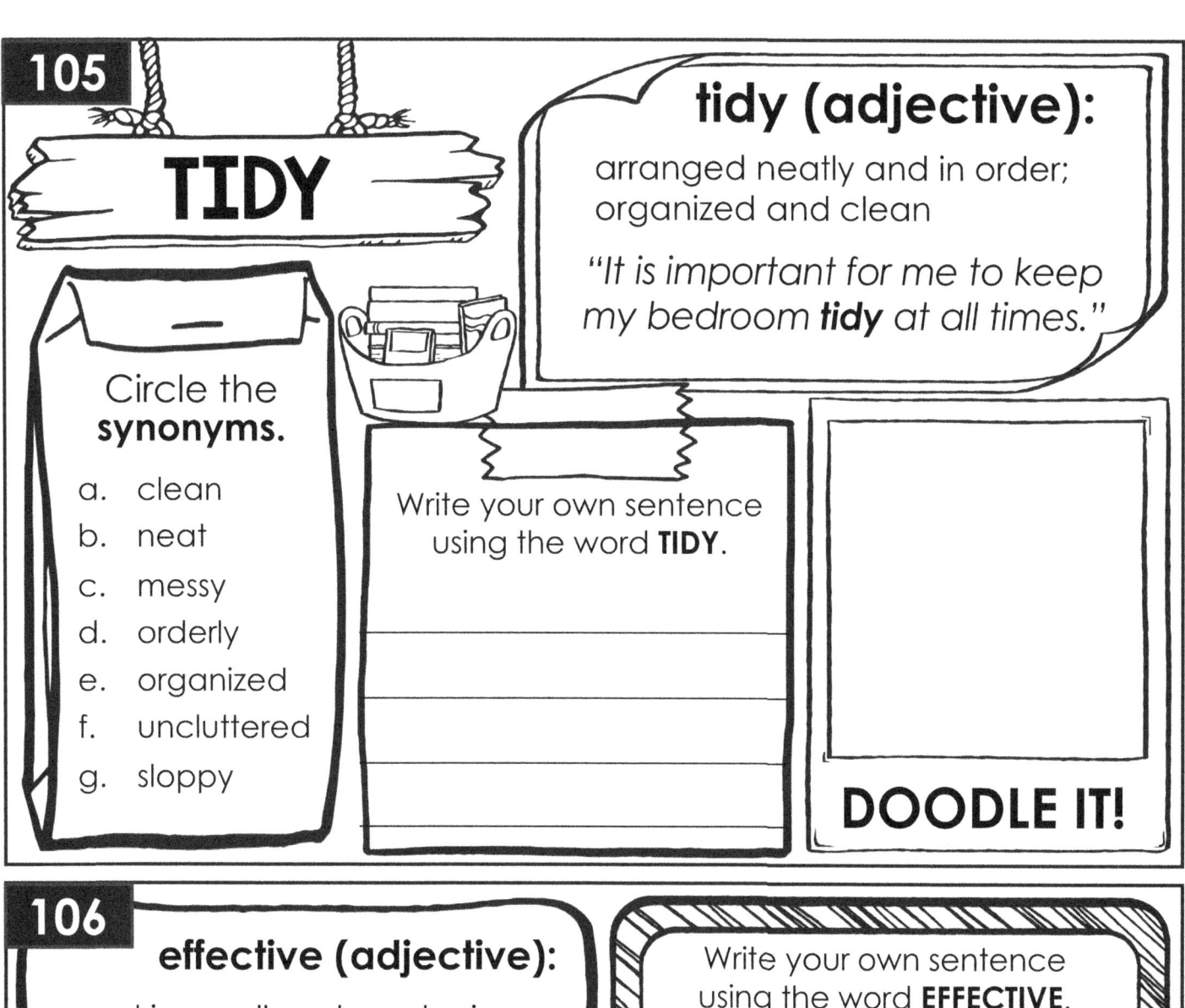

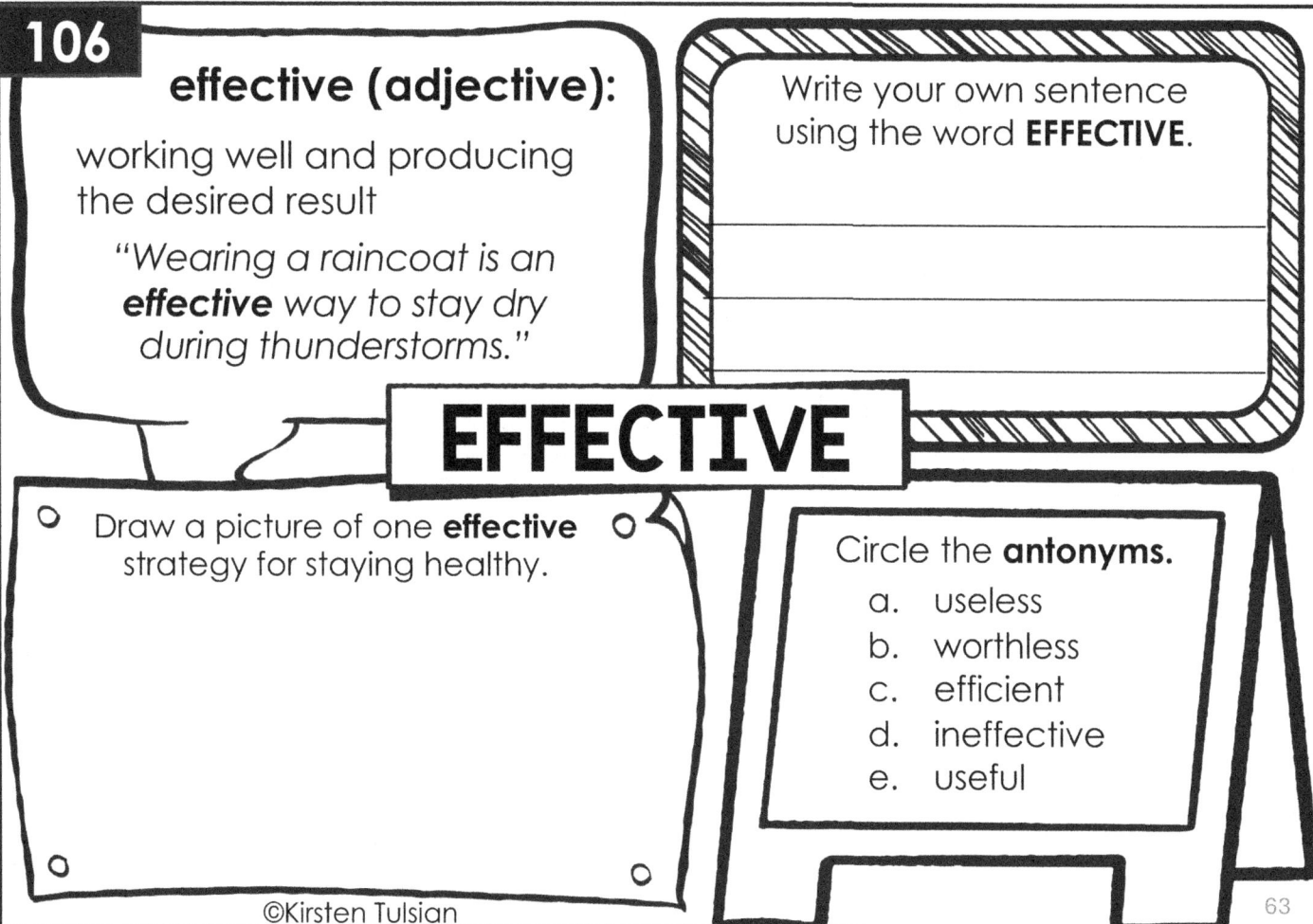

107

fabulous (adjective):

amazingly good or wonderful

"Our class had a fabulous time volunteering at the local animal shelter."

Draw a picture of a fabulous moment you've had this month.

FABULOUS

Write your own sentence using the word **FABULOUS**.

Circle the **synonyms**.
a. extraordinary
b. typical
c. incredible
d. marvelous
e. spectacular
f. ordinary

108

transform (verb):

to make a dramatic change in the form, look, or character of something

"You can transform the look of your bedroom with a fresh coat of paint."

Choose the best word to replace **TRANSFORMS** in the sentence below.

My sister has a toy that **transforms** from a robot into a truck.
a. remains   c. leaves
b. changes   d. preserves

TRANSFORM

Write your own sentence using the word **TRANSFORM**.

How does a butterfly **transform** during its lifetime? Draw one way.

109 tragic (adjective):

causing extreme sadness or distress, often involving an unexpected incident

*"I feel very sad about the **tragic** accident that happened near my house over the weekend."*

How can you help someone who's experienced a **tragic** event? Write two ways.

1.

2.

TRAGIC

Write your own sentence using the word **TRAGIC**.

Choose the best word to replace **TRAGIC** in the sentence below.

Our family suffered two **tragic** losses during the summer.

- a. comforting
- b. unimportant
- c. heartbreaking
- d. harmless

110 enable (verb):

to give someone the means or power to do something

*"The tool **enables** us to assemble the furniture quickly and easily."*

Choose the best word to replace **ENABLES** in the sentence below.

The flashlight **enables** me to see the path after it gets dark outside.

- a. allows
- b. prevents
- c. prohibits
- d. forbids

DOODLE IT!

ENABLE

Write your own sentence using the word **ENABLE**.

111

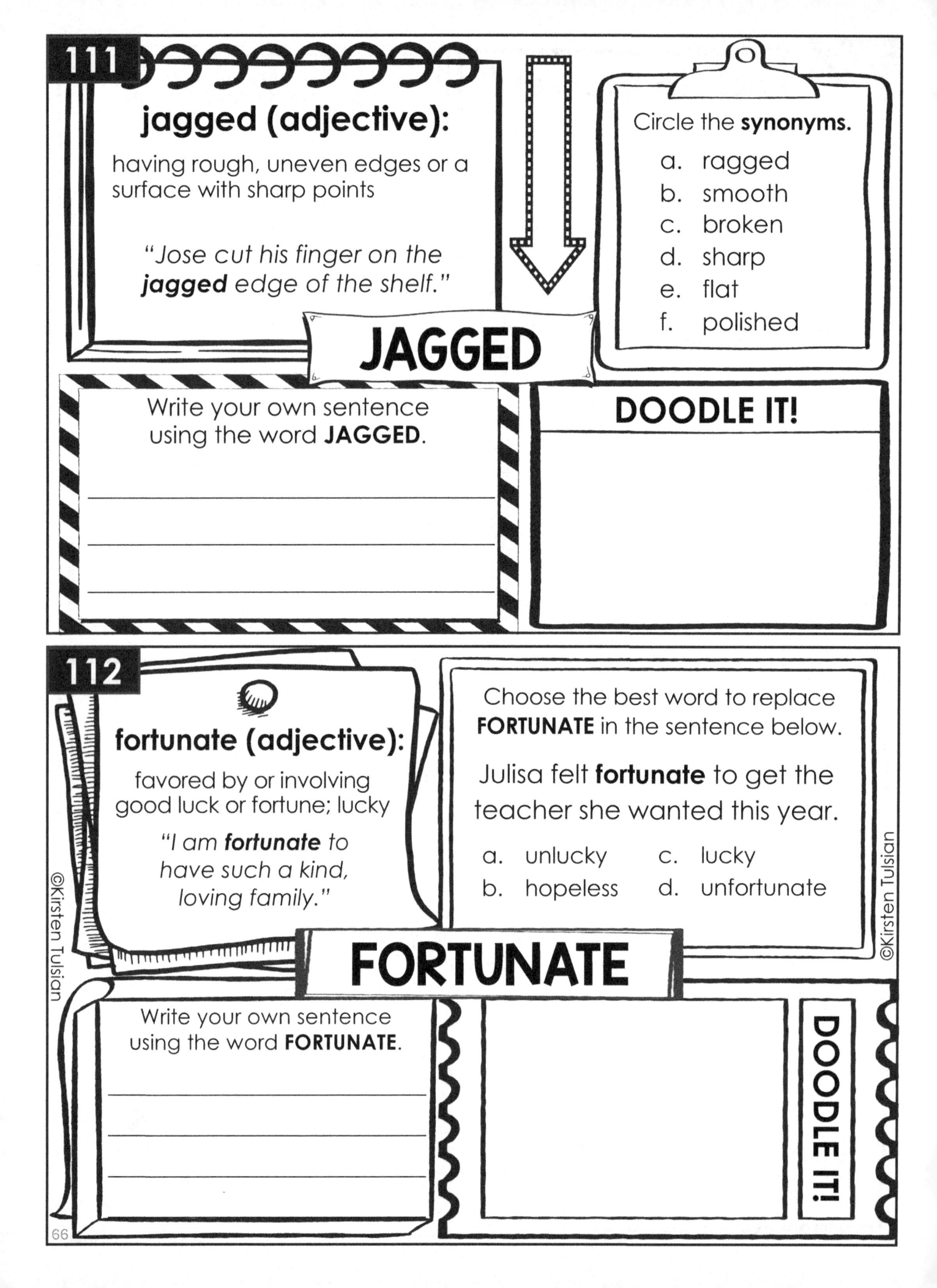

jagged (adjective):
having rough, uneven edges or a surface with sharp points

*"Jose cut his finger on the **jagged** edge of the shelf."*

JAGGED

Circle the **synonyms.**
a. ragged
b. smooth
c. broken
d. sharp
e. flat
f. polished

Write your own sentence using the word **JAGGED**.

DOODLE IT!

112

fortunate (adjective):
favored by or involving good luck or fortune; lucky

*"I am **fortunate** to have such a kind, loving family."*

FORTUNATE

Choose the best word to replace **FORTUNATE** in the sentence below.

Julisa felt **fortunate** to get the teacher she wanted this year.

a. unlucky   c. lucky
b. hopeless   d. unfortunate

Write your own sentence using the word **FORTUNATE**.

DOODLE IT!

113 EXPAND

expand (verb): to become larger or more extensive; to make something bigger or wider

*"The narrow path through the woods **expanded** into a wide road."*

Circle the **synonyms.**
a. enlarge
b. widen
c. decrease
d. broaden
e. narrow
f. grow
g. shrink

Write your own sentence using the word **EXPAND**.

DOODLE IT!

114 INDULGE

indulge (verb): to give into something one really wants or enjoys; to allow oneself a particular pleasure

*"After a big test, I like to **indulge** in a big bowl of ice cream."*

Write your own sentence using the word **INDULGE**.

What are three things you like to **indulge** in every now and then?
1.
2.
3.

Circle the **antonyms.**
a. satisfy
b. deprive
c. neglect
d. enjoy
e. refrain

©Kirsten Tulsian

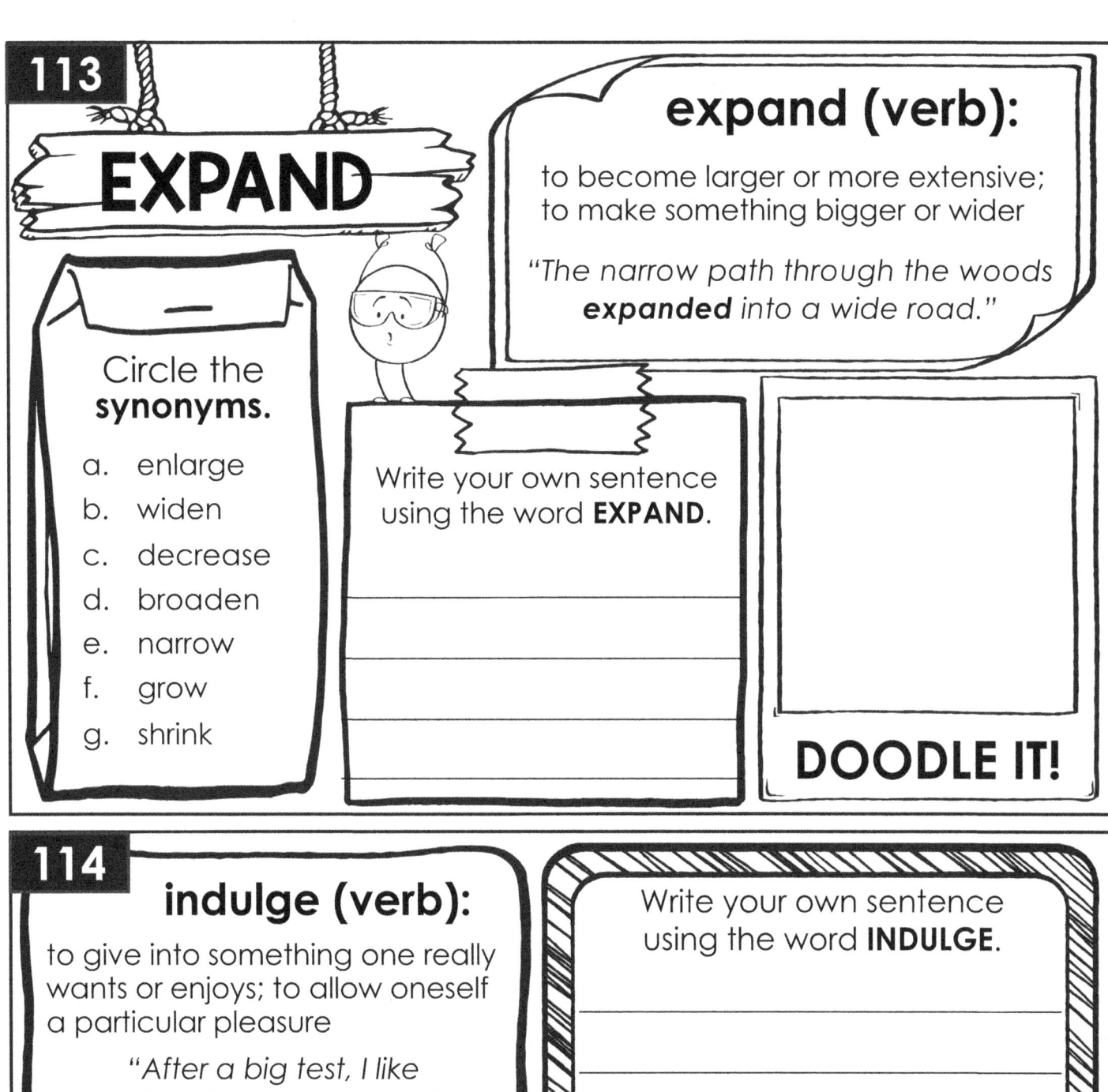

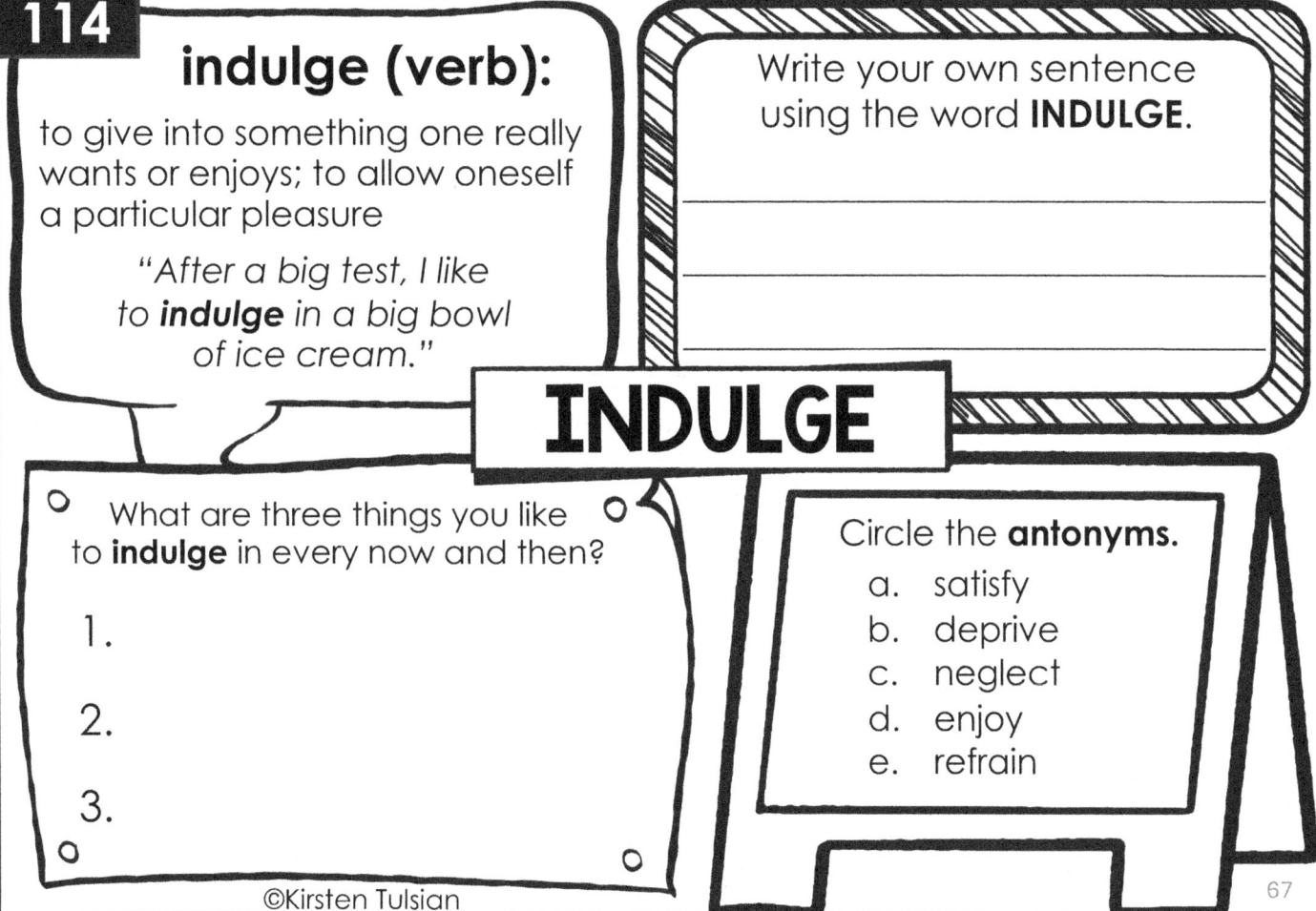

115

envy (noun):

a resentful or jealous feeling toward someone else's possessions, qualities, or luck

*"My new puppy was the **envy** of all my friends."*

Draw a picture of a time when you felt **ENVY**.

ENVY

Write your own sentence using the word **ENVY**.

Circle the **synonyms**.
a. resentment
b. comfort
c. pleasure
d. jealousy
e. longing
f. loving

116

tender (adjective):

gentle; with concern or sympathy; (of food) easy to cut or chew

*"She has an incredible soft spot and **tender** heart for animals."*

Choose the best word to replace **TENDER** in the sentence below.

Abigail's **tender** smile lit up the entire room.
a. loving   c. vicious
b. tough   d. uncertain

TENDER

Write your own sentence using the word **TENDER**.

DOODLE IT!

117

hazy (adjective):

unclear, misty, foggy, or smoky

"A **hazy** blanket of fog rested on the valley."

Draw a picture of **hazy** mountaintops.

HAZY

Write your own sentence using the word **HAZY**.

Circle the **synonyms**.
a. sunny
b. smoggy
c. murky
d. clear
e. clouded
f. misty

118

linger (verb):

to stay in a place longer than necessary; to be slow to disappear

"The heat **lingered** long after the sun had gone down."

Choose the best word to replace **LINGERED** in the sentence below.

The nightmare I had last night **lingered** in my mind for several hours.

a. departed   c. discontinued
b. hurried   d. remained

DOODLE IT!

LINGER

Write your own sentence using the word **LINGER**.

119

blunder (noun):

a stupid or careless mistake; words that come out in a clumsy way

*"She stopped talking after she realized the **blunder** she'd made."*

BLUNDER

Circle the **synonyms.**
a. perfection
b. mistake
c. error
d. blooper
e. success
f. accuracy

Write your own sentence using the word **BLUNDER**.

DOODLE IT!

120

perish (verb):

to die or be destroyed; to suffer complete ruin or destruction

*"When the frost comes, most flowers **perish**."*

PERISH

Choose the best word to replace **PERISHED** in the sentence below.

Many ancient languages have **perished** over time.

a. flourished
b. disappeared
c. revived
d. thrived

Write your own sentence using the word **PERISH**.

DOODLE IT!

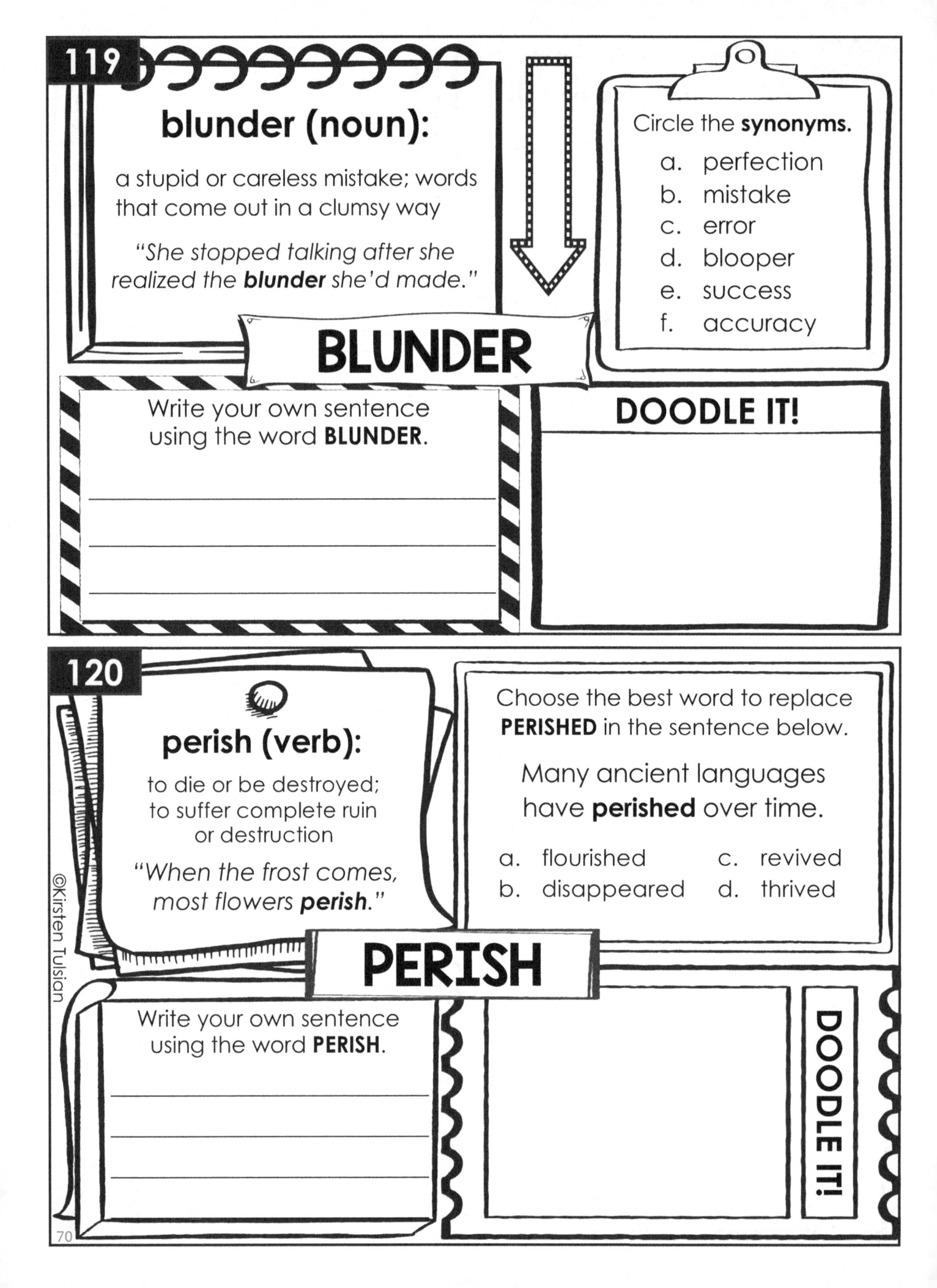

©Kirsten Tulsian

121

PLEAD

plead (verb): to offer or ask for something in a very serious and emotional way

*"My little sister **pleaded** with me not to tell on her."*

Circle the **synonyms.**
a. refuse
b. request
c. beg
d. punish
e. ask
f. laugh
g. convince

Write your own sentence using the word **PLEAD**.

DOODLE IT!

122

avoid (verb): to keep away from or to stop oneself from doing something

*"The only reason I didn't go to the concert was to **avoid** the big crowds."*

AVOID

Write your own sentence using the word **AVOID**.

Draw a picture of something you generally try to **AVOID**.

Circle the **antonyms.**
a. escape
b. dodge
c. seek out
d. embrace
e. welcome

123

hostile (adjective): unfriendly and perhaps considered mean

"My dad left his job because of the hostile work environment."

Briefly describe a time when someone was **hostile** to you.

HOSTILE

Write your own sentence using the word **HOSTILE**.

Circle the **synonyms**.
a. kind
b. mean
c. hateful
d. loving
e. nasty
f. understanding

124

fiasco (noun): a plan that goes wrong and is a failure, sometimes in an embarrassing way

"The unexpected rain turned the party into a total fiasco."

Choose the best word to replace **FIASCO** in the sentence below.
Getting through airport security with a baby stroller can feel like a **fiasco**.
a. winner
b. benefit
c. disaster
d. miracle

FIASCO

Circle the **synonyms**.
a. disaster
b. achievement
c. failure
d. win
e. catastrophe
f. success

Write your own sentence using the word **FIASCO**.

DOODLE IT!

©Kirsten Tulsian

125 arid (adjective):

very dry, like a desert, with little or no rain

*"Without rainfall, most flowers cannot thrive in an **arid** climate."*

ARID

DOODLE IT!

Write your own sentence using the word **ARID**.

Choose the best word to replace **ARID** in the sentence below.

Because camels store water, they are well-suited for **arid** areas.

a. moist
b. humid
c. damp
d. parched

126 wrangle (verb):

to have a long and complicated dispute or fight over something

*"My mom **wrangled** with the neighbor about the noise level coming from their house."*

Choose the best word to replace **WRANGLE** in the sentence below.

I always **wrangle** with my aunt about bedtime when I sleep at her house.

a. understand
b. arrange
c. squabble
d. agree

DOODLE IT!

WRANGLE

Write your own sentence using the word **WRANGLE**.

©Kirsten Tulsian

127

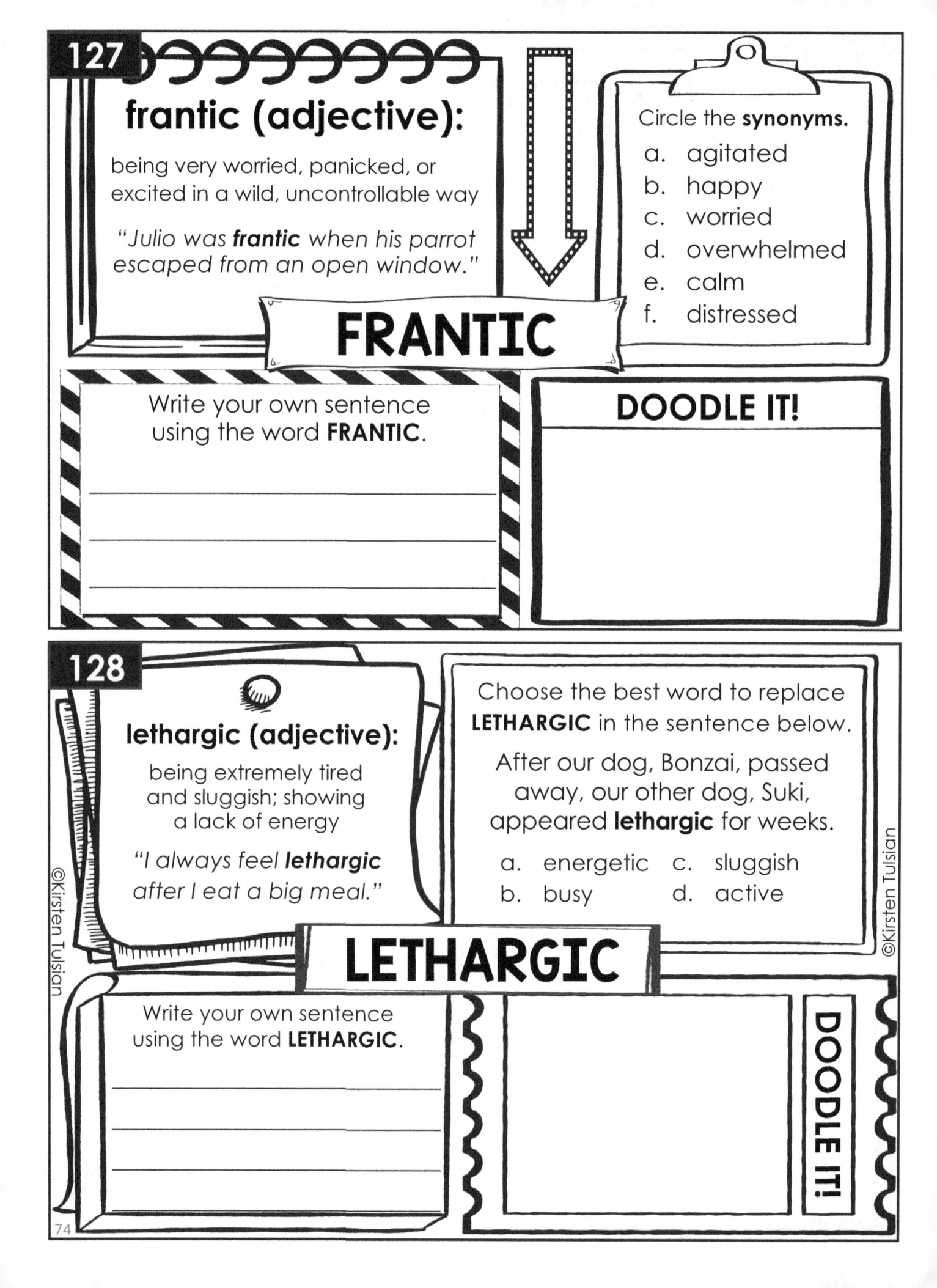

frantic (adjective):

being very worried, panicked, or excited in a wild, uncontrollable way

"Julio was **frantic** when his parrot escaped from an open window."

Circle the **synonyms**.
a. agitated
b. happy
c. worried
d. overwhelmed
e. calm
f. distressed

FRANTIC

Write your own sentence using the word **FRANTIC**.

DOODLE IT!

128

lethargic (adjective):

being extremely tired and sluggish; showing a lack of energy

"I always feel **lethargic** after I eat a big meal."

Choose the best word to replace **LETHARGIC** in the sentence below.

After our dog, Bonzai, passed away, our other dog, Suki, appeared **lethargic** for weeks.

a. energetic
b. busy
c. sluggish
d. active

LETHARGIC

Write your own sentence using the word **LETHARGIC**.

DOODLE IT!

129

SWARM

swarm (noun):

a dense group of flying insects

*"The sky went dark, and a huge **swarm** of locusts circled overhead."*

Circle the **synonyms**.

a. flock
b. crowd
c. loner
d. herd
e. individual
f. group
g. creature

Write your own sentence using the word **SWARM**.

DOODLE IT!

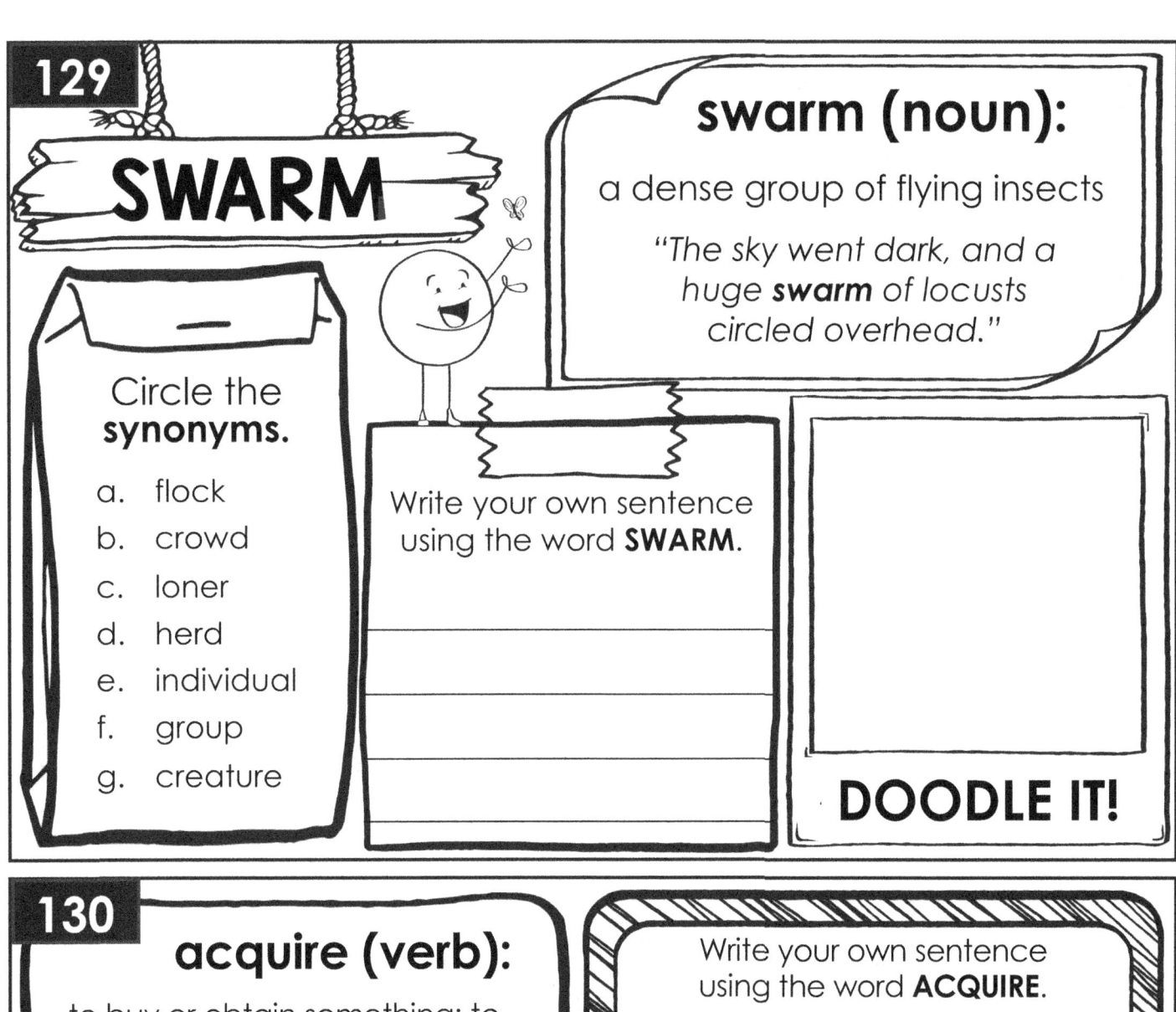

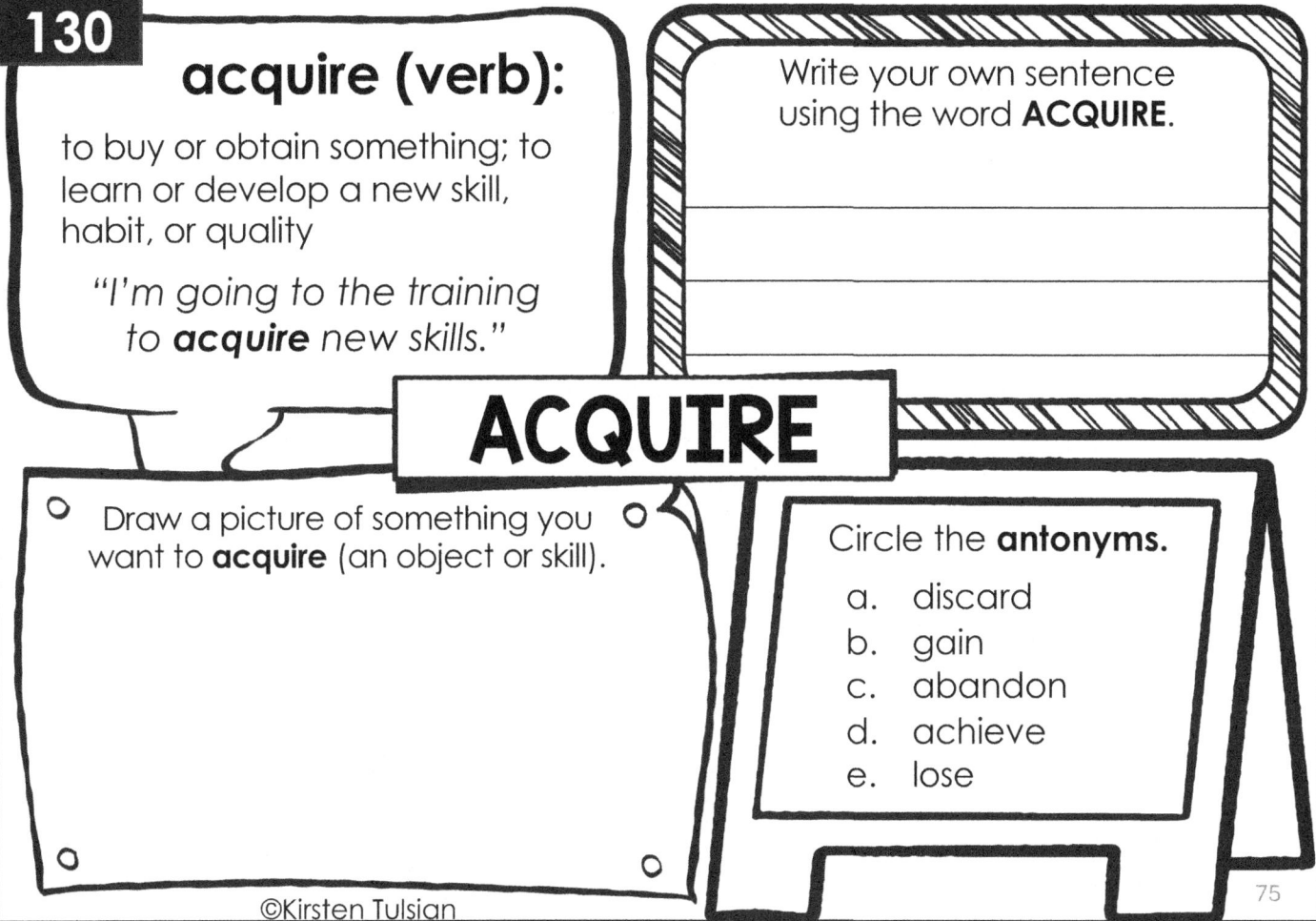

130

acquire (verb):

to buy or obtain something; to learn or develop a new skill, habit, or quality

*"I'm going to the training to **acquire** new skills."*

Write your own sentence using the word **ACQUIRE**.

ACQUIRE

Draw a picture of something you want to **acquire** (an object or skill).

Circle the **antonyms**.

a. discard
b. gain
c. abandon
d. achieve
e. lose

131

abandon (verb):
to leave something or someone; to give up an action, practice, or way of thinking

"The approaching fire forced residents to abandon their homes."

Briefly describe a habit or activity you'd like to **abandon**.
_____
_____
_____

ABANDON

Write your own sentence using the word **ABANDON**.
_____
_____
_____

Circle the **synonyms**.
a. leave
b. embrace
c. dump
d. keep
e. ditch
f. discard

132

anxious (adjective):
feeling worried, nervous, or uneasy, usually about something that might happen

"I feel anxious about the soccer tryouts after school."

Choose the best word to replace **ANXIOUS** in the sentence below.

He felt **anxious** that it might rain during his birthday party.

a. sure   c. happy
b. uneasy d. unafraid

ANXIOUS

Circle the **antonyms**.
a. calm
b. relaxed
c. worried
d. confident
e. nervous
f. troubled

Write your own sentence using the word **ANXIOUS**.
_____
_____
_____

DOODLE IT!

©Kirsten Tulsian

133

empathy (noun):

the ability to share and understand the feelings of another

*"Showing **empathy** for someone else's struggles shows great character."*

Draw a picture of a time when you had **empathy** for someone.

EMPATHY

Write your own sentence using the word **EMPATHY**.

Circle the **synonyms.**
a. sympathy
b. hatred
c. understanding
d. compassion
e. indifference
f. cruelty

134

feeble (adjective):

lacking physical strength, especially because of age or illness; a soft or faint sound

*"After she had surgery, she felt tired and **feeble**."*

Choose the best word to replace **FEEBLE** in the sentence below.

The **feeble** old man struggled to stand up from his chair.

a. fragile   c. strong
b. powerful   d. athletic

DOODLE IT!

FEEBLE

Write your own sentence using the word **FEEBLE**.

©Kirsten Tulsian

135

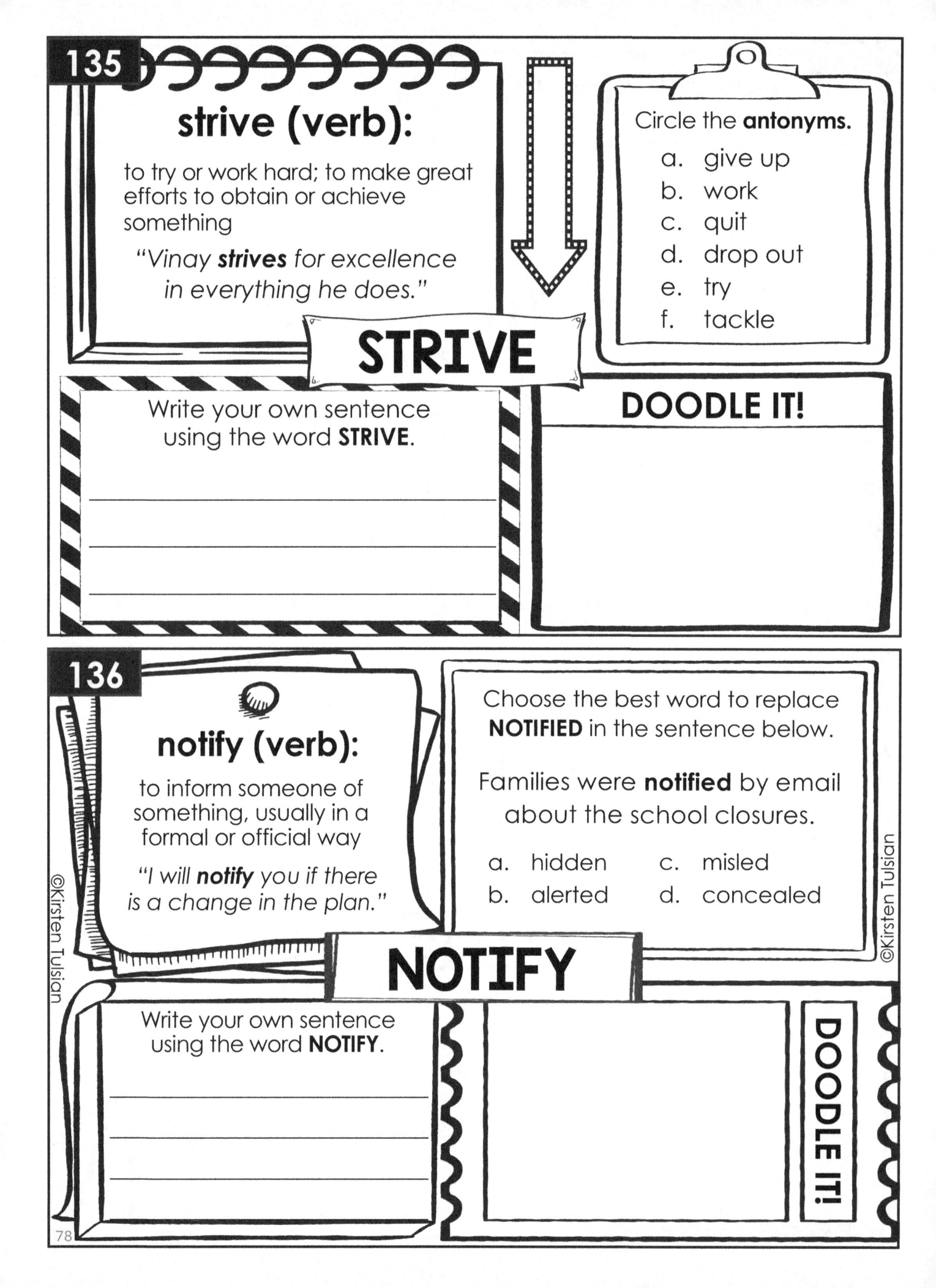

strive (verb):

to try or work hard; to make great efforts to obtain or achieve something

*"Vinay **strives** for excellence in everything he does."*

STRIVE

Circle the **antonyms**.
a. give up
b. work
c. quit
d. drop out
e. try
f. tackle

Write your own sentence using the word **STRIVE**.

DOODLE IT!

136

notify (verb):

to inform someone of something, usually in a formal or official way

*"I will **notify** you if there is a change in the plan."*

NOTIFY

Choose the best word to replace **NOTIFIED** in the sentence below.

Families were **notified** by email about the school closures.

a. hidden   c. misled
b. alerted   d. concealed

Write your own sentence using the word **NOTIFY**.

DOODLE IT!

137 UNRULY

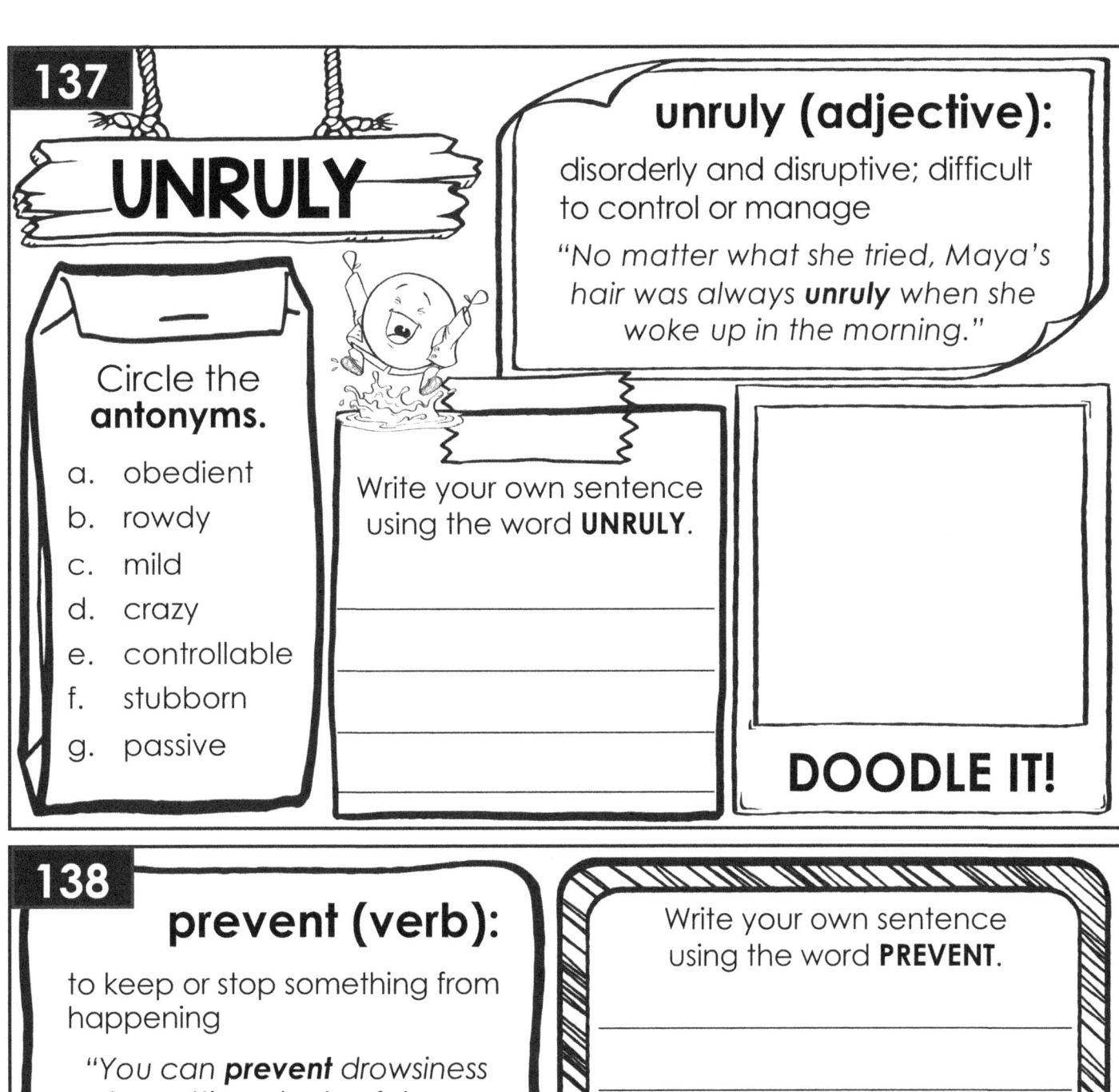

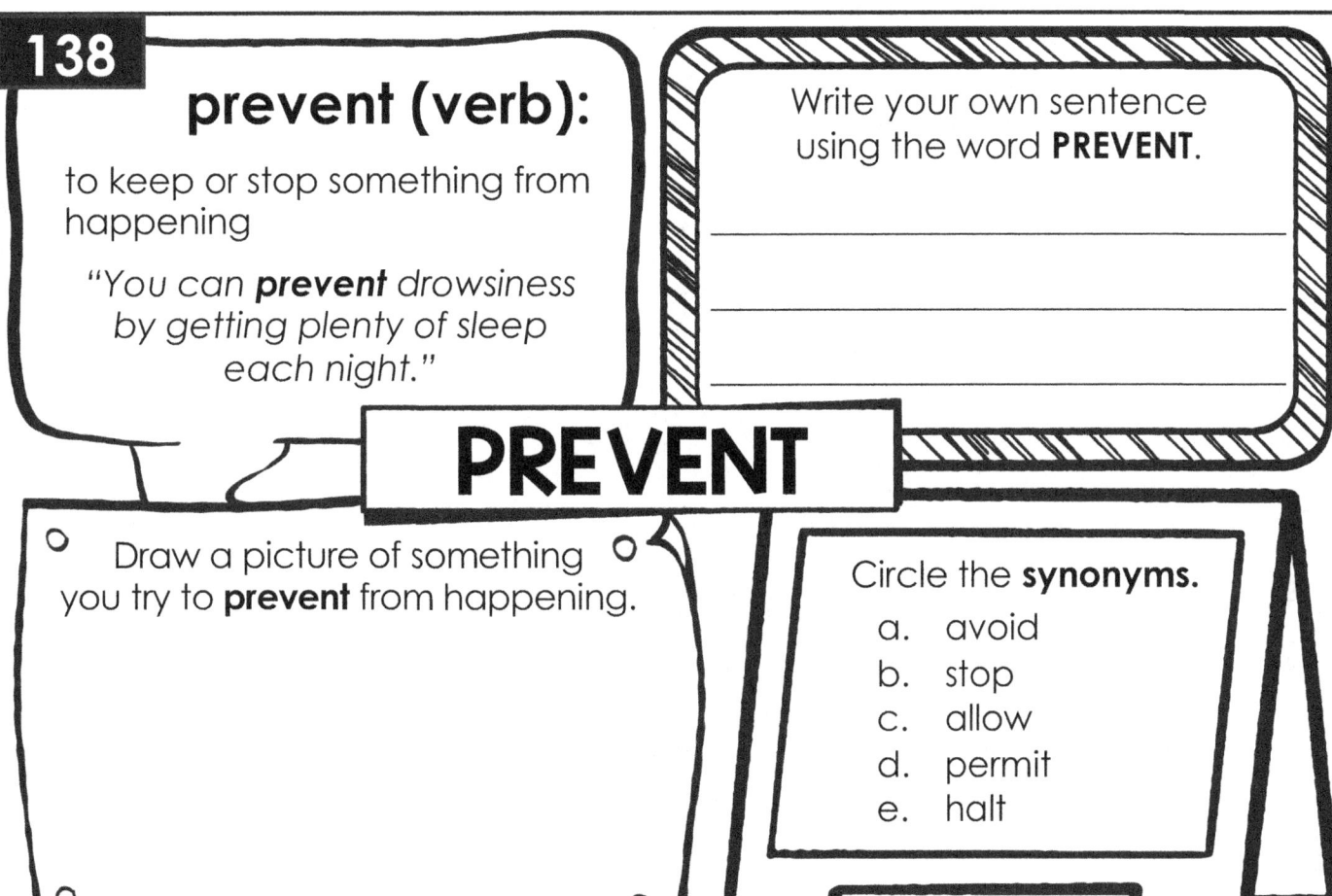

unruly (adjective): disorderly and disruptive; difficult to control or manage

*"No matter what she tried, Maya's hair was always **unruly** when she woke up in the morning."*

Circle the **antonyms.**
a. obedient
b. rowdy
c. mild
d. crazy
e. controllable
f. stubborn
g. passive

Write your own sentence using the word **UNRULY**.

DOODLE IT!

138 PREVENT

prevent (verb): to keep or stop something from happening

*"You can **prevent** drowsiness by getting plenty of sleep each night."*

Write your own sentence using the word **PREVENT**.

Draw a picture of something you try to **prevent** from happening.

Circle the **synonyms.**
a. avoid
b. stop
c. allow
d. permit
e. halt

139

sensitive (adjective): quick to feel or detect slight changes; having a delicate appreciation of others' feelings; perceptive

"Jimmy acts tough, but he's a deeply sensitive boy."

What do you feel **sensitive** toward? Draw a picture.

SENSITIVE

Write your own sentence using the word **SENSITIVE**.

Circle the **synonyms.**
a. unaware
b. perceptive
c. responsive
d. numb
e. understanding
f. heartless

140

mimic (verb): to imitate someone's words or actions, often to entertain or make fun of

"Many parrots can mimic the voices of their owners."

Choose the best word to replace **MIMIC** in the sentence below.

When Benny screams, his little sister **mimics** every sound.
a. prevents   c. silences
b. halts   d. imitates

MIMIC

Circle the **synonyms.**
a. copy
b. prevent
c. imitate
d. mock
e. stop

Write your own sentence using the word **MIMIC**.

©Kirsten Tulsian

141

recycle (verb):

to convert waste or garbage into reusable material; to use again

"My uncle **recycles** bolts, screws, and washers into art pieces."

DOODLE IT!

RECYCLE

Write your own sentence using the word **RECYCLE**.

Choose the best word(s) to replace **RECYCLE** in the sentence below.

You can wash and **recycle** sour cream containers to store food.

a. throw away
b. dump
c. toss
d. reuse

142

pursue (verb):

to follow someone or something in order to catch or achieve it

"A cat will patiently **pursue** a mouse until it's caught."

Choose the best word to replace **PURSUE** in the sentence below.

It is important to **pursue** your dreams and aspirations in life!

a. hide
b. lose
c. neglect
d. chase

PURSUE

Draw a picture of a dream or goal you want to **pursue**.

Write your own sentence using the word **PURSUE**.

©Kirsten Tulsian

143

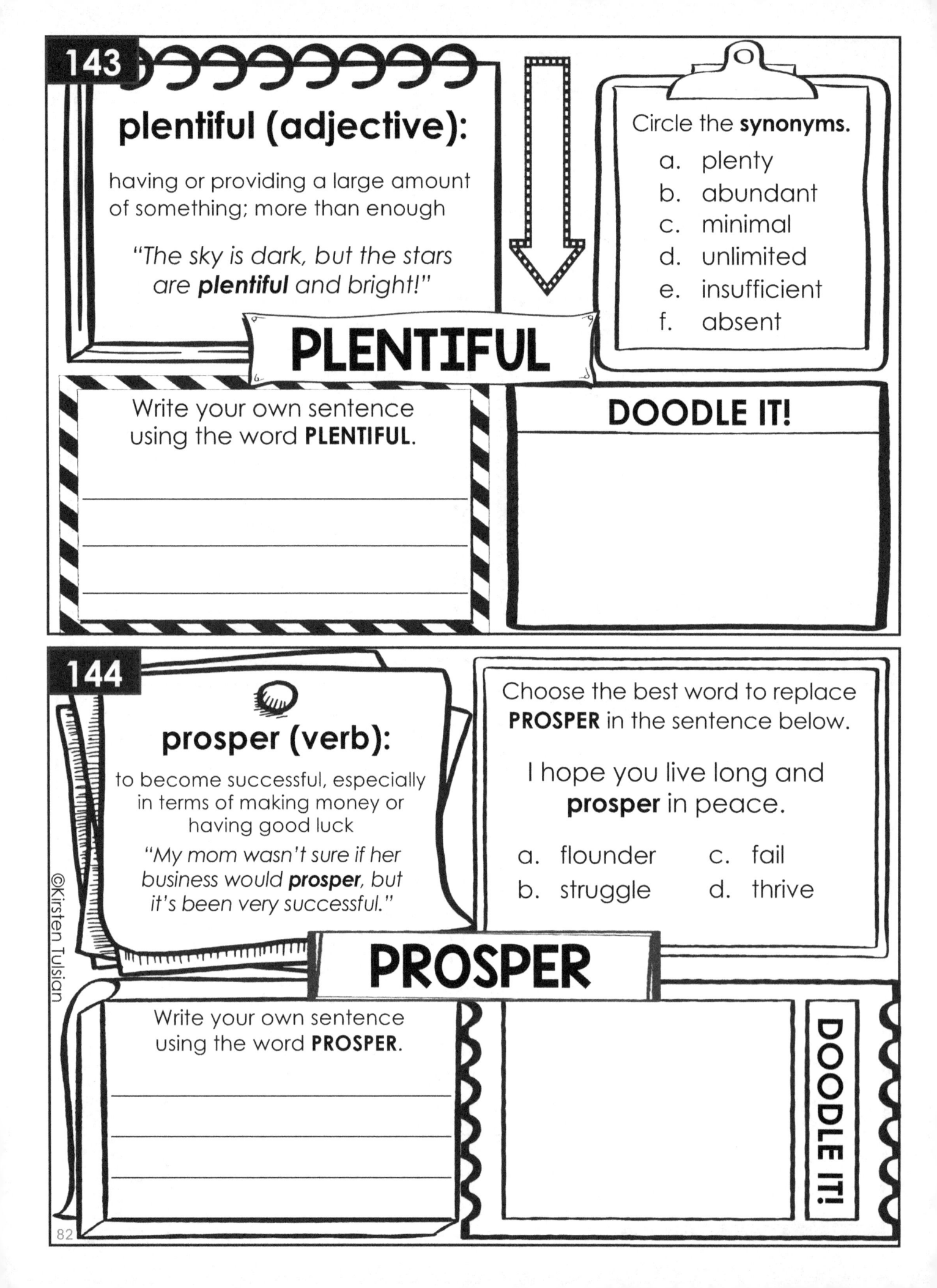

plentiful (adjective):

having or providing a large amount of something; more than enough

*"The sky is dark, but the stars are **plentiful** and bright!"*

PLENTIFUL

Circle the **synonyms.**
a. plenty
b. abundant
c. minimal
d. unlimited
e. insufficient
f. absent

Write your own sentence using the word **PLENTIFUL.**

DOODLE IT!

144

prosper (verb):

to become successful, especially in terms of making money or having good luck

*"My mom wasn't sure if her business would **prosper**, but it's been very successful."*

PROSPER

Choose the best word to replace **PROSPER** in the sentence below.

I hope you live long and **prosper** in peace.

a. flounder   c. fail
b. struggle   d. thrive

Write your own sentence using the word **PROSPER.**

DOODLE IT!

145

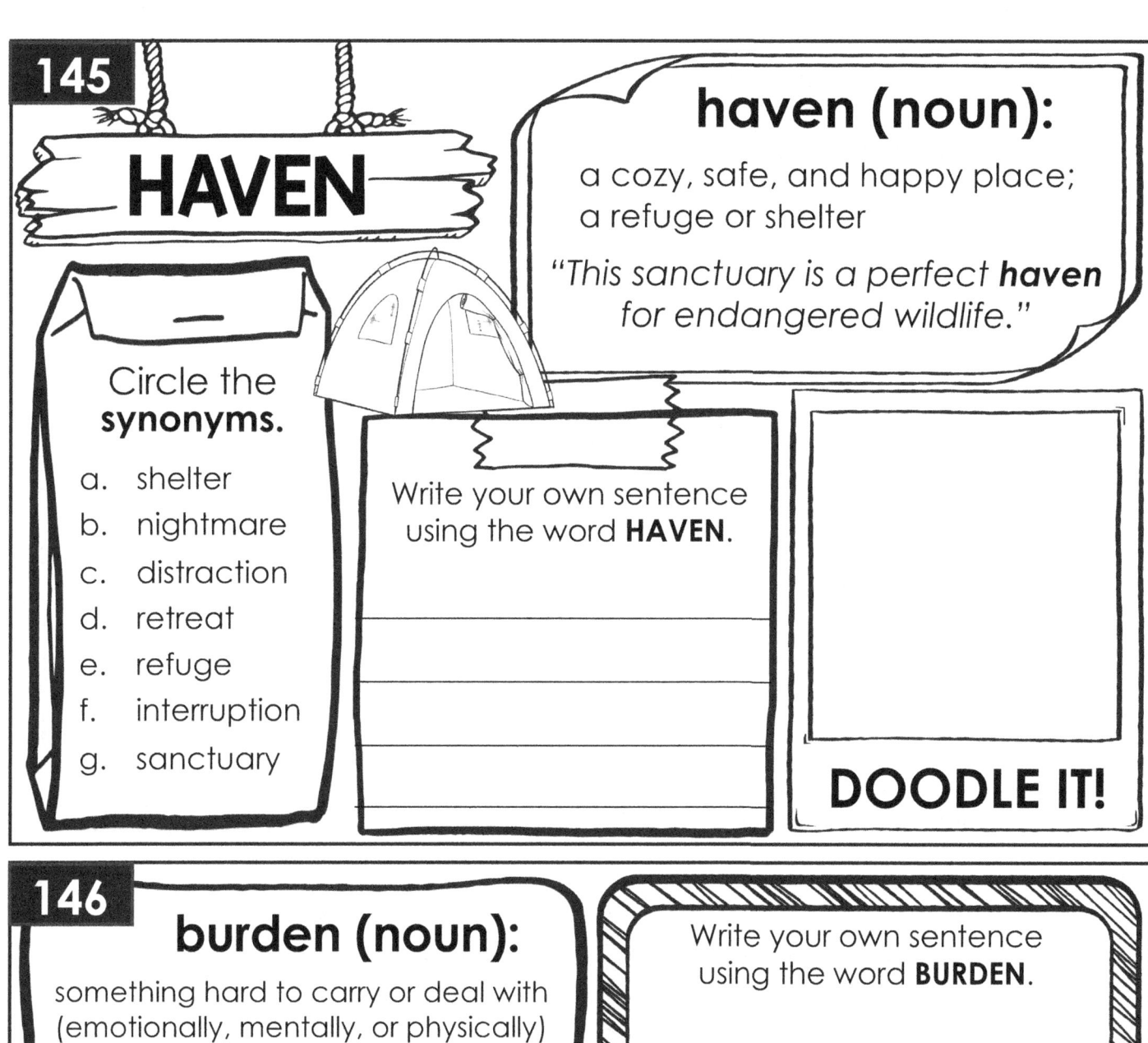

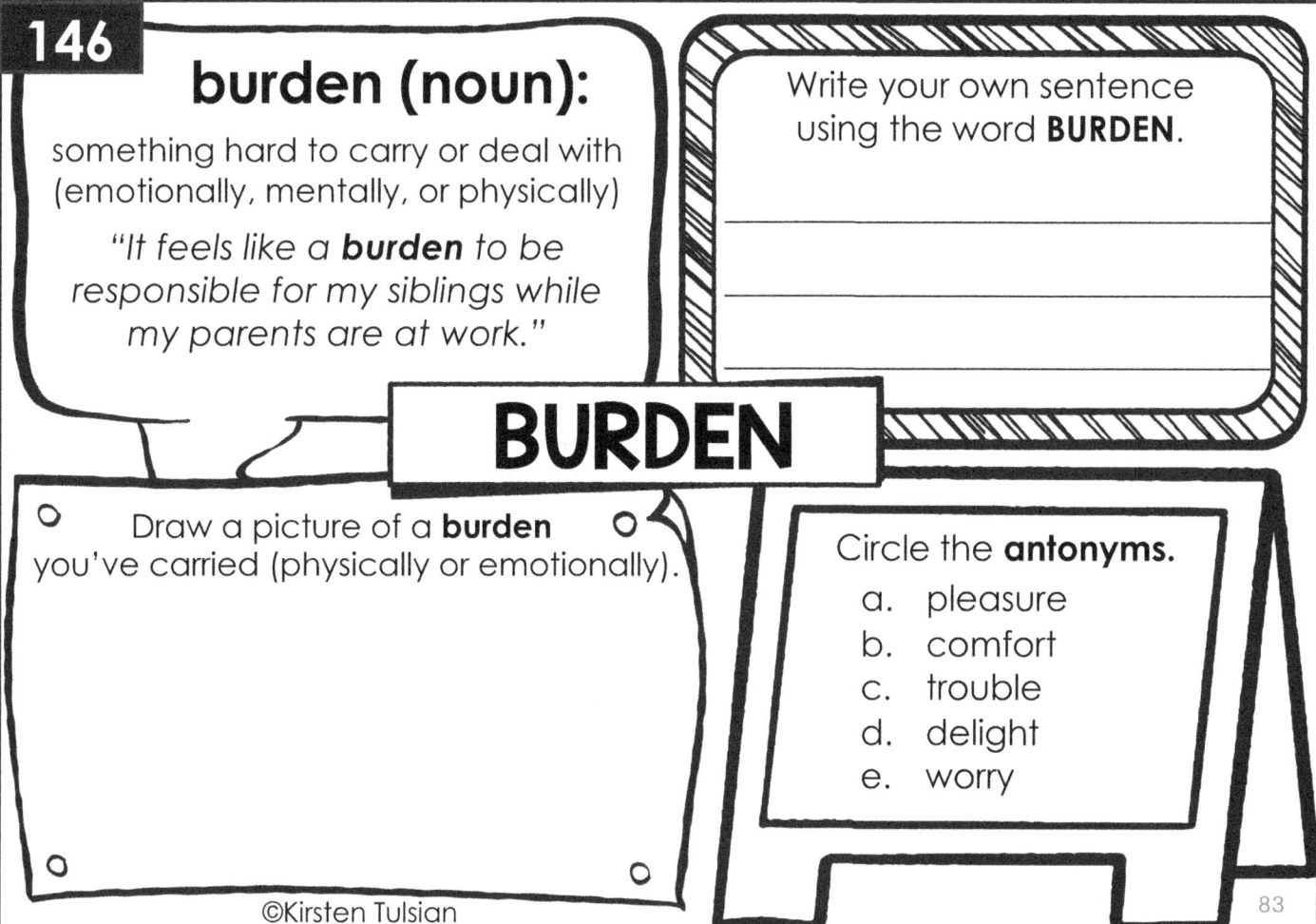

HAVEN

haven (noun):
a cozy, safe, and happy place; a refuge or shelter

"This sanctuary is a perfect haven for endangered wildlife."

Circle the **synonyms**.
a. shelter
b. nightmare
c. distraction
d. retreat
e. refuge
f. interruption
g. sanctuary

Write your own sentence using the word **HAVEN**.

DOODLE IT!

146

burden (noun):
something hard to carry or deal with (emotionally, mentally, or physically)

"It feels like a burden to be responsible for my siblings while my parents are at work."

BURDEN

Write your own sentence using the word **BURDEN**.

Draw a picture of a **burden** you've carried (physically or emotionally).

Circle the **antonyms**.
a. pleasure
b. comfort
c. trouble
d. delight
e. worry

147

dazzle (verb):
to impress with something beautiful, amazing, or bright

"I will dazzle you with my artistic and creative abilities."

Draw a picture of something that **dazzles** you.

DAZZLE

Write your own sentence using the word **DAZZLE**.

Circle the **synonyms**.
a. astonish
b. disappoint
c. excite
d. impress
e. surprise
f. bore

148

clarify (verb):
to make something less confusing and easier to understand

"I want to clarify what I said about the rules in the library."

Choose the best word to replace **CLARIFY** in the sentence below.

Please **clarify** what you meant when you said the tests will be confusing.
a. avoid
b. forget
c. explain
d. ignore

CLARIFY

Write your own sentence using the word **CLARIFY**.

DOODLE IT!

149

contribute (verb):

to help achieve or provide something

*"Volunteers **contribute** so much time and energy to support causes that matter to them."*

How can you **contribute** to the betterment of your community? Write two ways.

1.

2.

CONTRIBUTE

Write your own sentence using the word **CONTRIBUTE**.

Choose the best word to replace **CONTRIBUTE** in the sentence below.

You need to **contribute** $20.00 to be a member of the organization.

  a. keep
  b. donate
  c. hold
  d. save

150

doze (verb):

to sleep lightly; to nap

*"I was just about to **doze** off when my uncle called."*

Choose the best word to replace **DOZING** in the sentence below.

The ducks relaxed under the shaded tree, **dozing** on and off.

  a. screaming   c. playing
  b. singing   d. sleeping

DOODLE IT!

DOZE

Write your own sentence using the word **DOZE**.

151

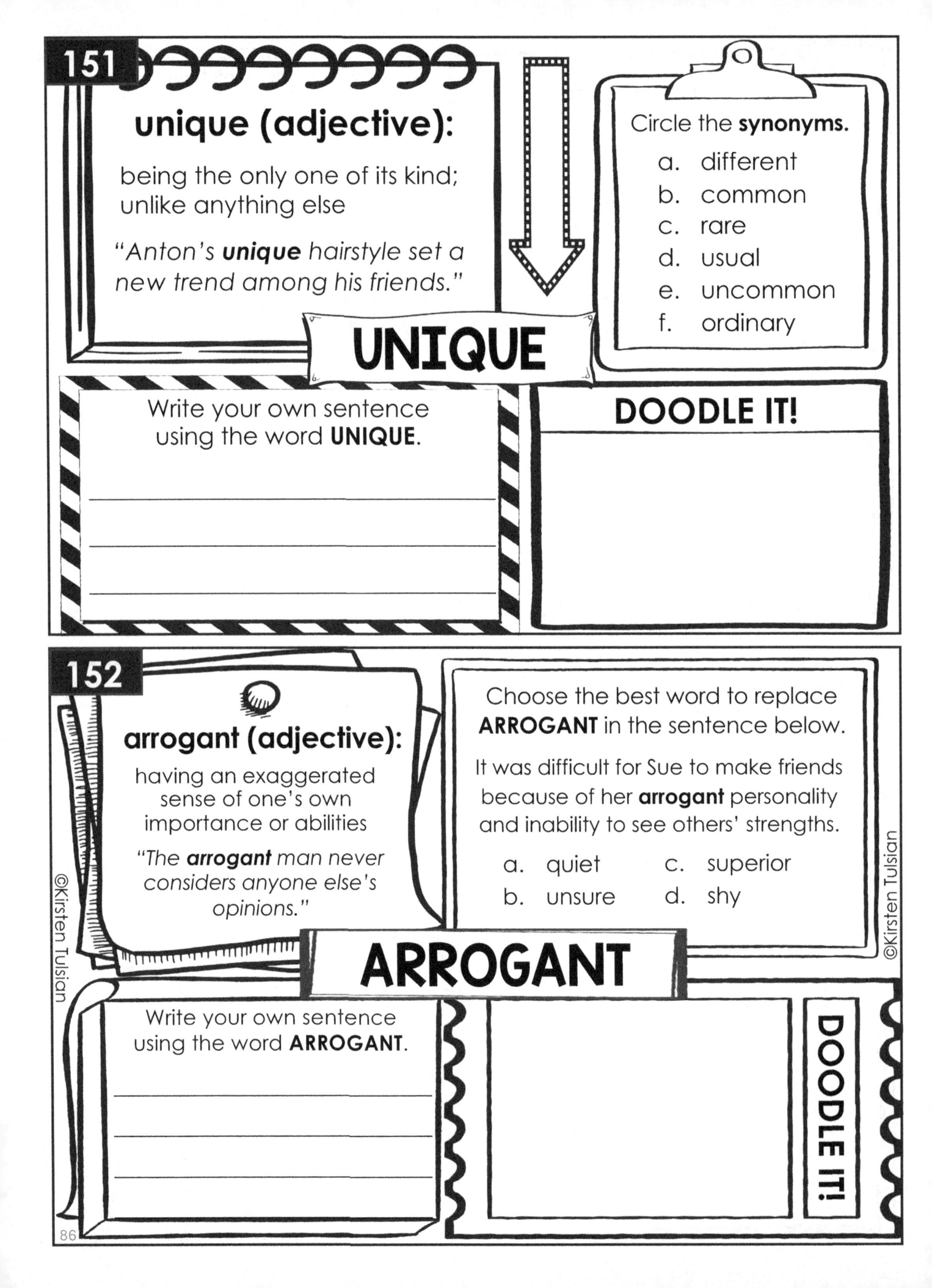

unique (adjective):

being the only one of its kind; unlike anything else

"Anton's **unique** hairstyle set a new trend among his friends."

UNIQUE

Circle the **synonyms**.
a. different
b. common
c. rare
d. usual
e. uncommon
f. ordinary

Write your own sentence using the word **UNIQUE**.

DOODLE IT!

152

arrogant (adjective):

having an exaggerated sense of one's own importance or abilities

"The **arrogant** man never considers anyone else's opinions."

ARROGANT

Choose the best word to replace **ARROGANT** in the sentence below.

It was difficult for Sue to make friends because of her **arrogant** personality and inability to see others' strengths.

a. quiet
b. unsure
c. superior
d. shy

Write your own sentence using the word **ARROGANT**.

DOODLE IT!

153

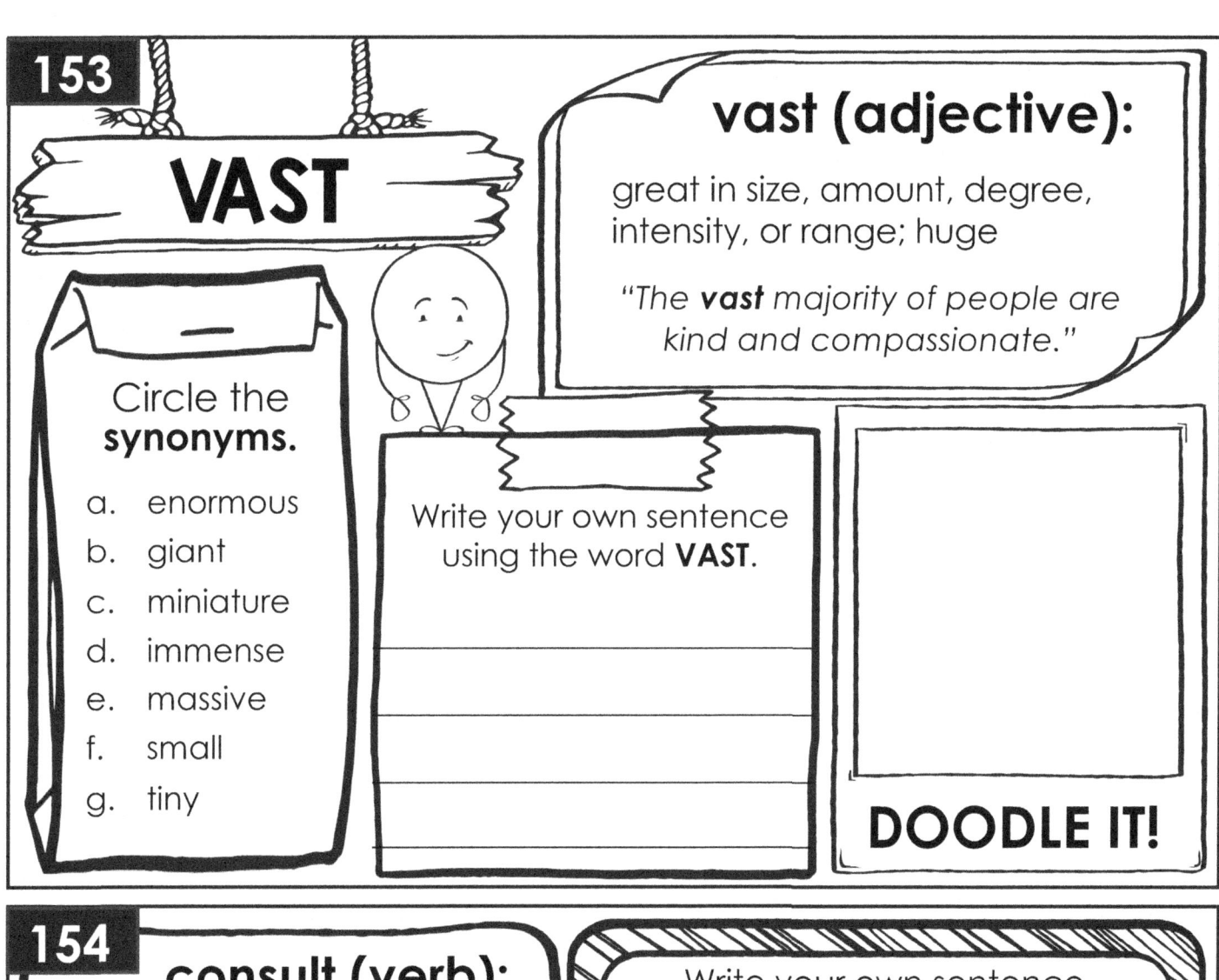

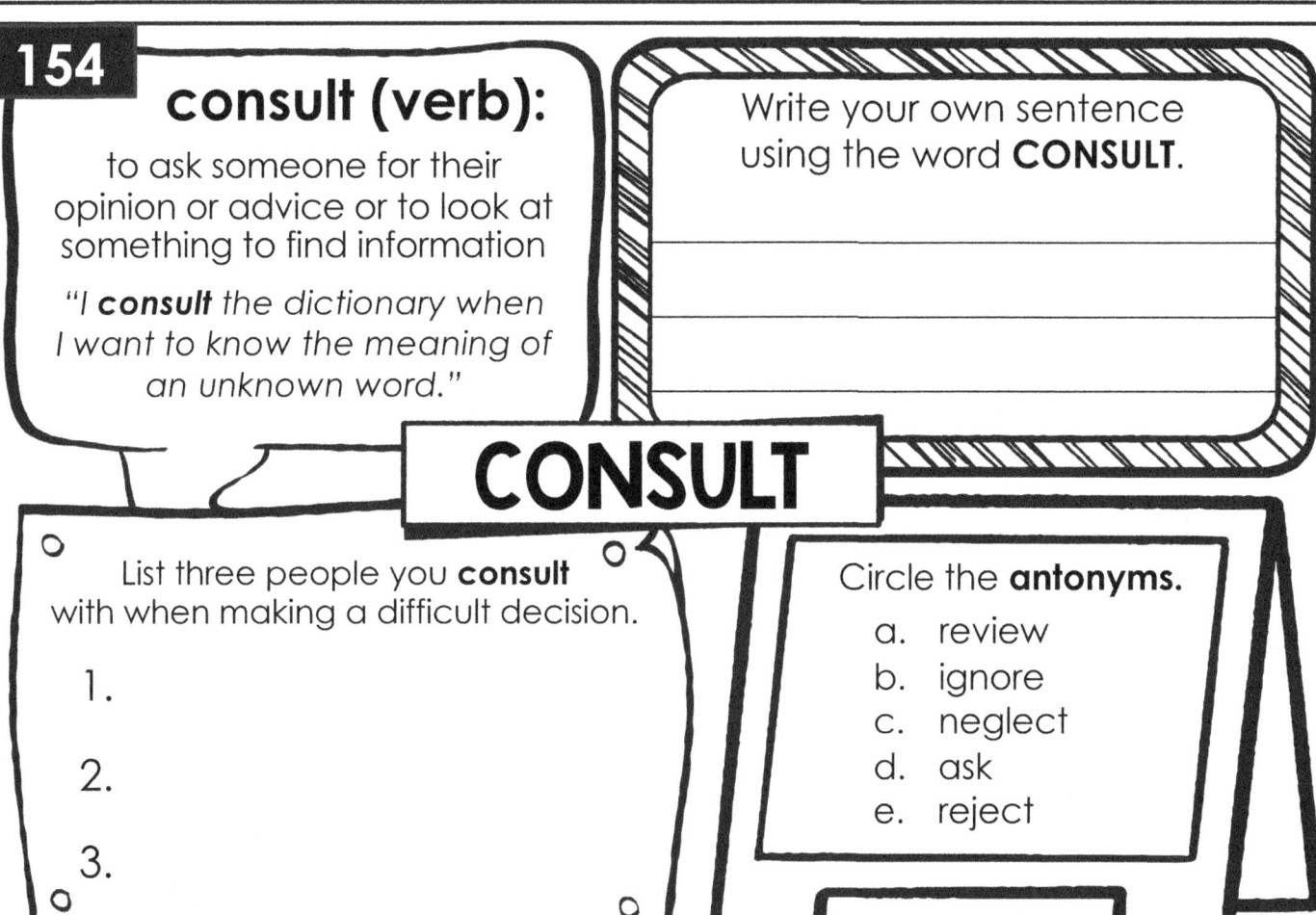

VAST

vast (adjective):

great in size, amount, degree, intensity, or range; huge

*"The **vast** majority of people are kind and compassionate."*

Circle the **synonyms.**

a. enormous
b. giant
c. miniature
d. immense
e. massive
f. small
g. tiny

Write your own sentence using the word **VAST**.

DOODLE IT!

154

consult (verb):

to ask someone for their opinion or advice or to look at something to find information

*"I **consult** the dictionary when I want to know the meaning of an unknown word."*

Write your own sentence using the word **CONSULT**.

CONSULT

List three people you **consult** with when making a difficult decision.

1.
2.
3.

Circle the **antonyms.**

a. review
b. ignore
c. neglect
d. ask
e. reject

155

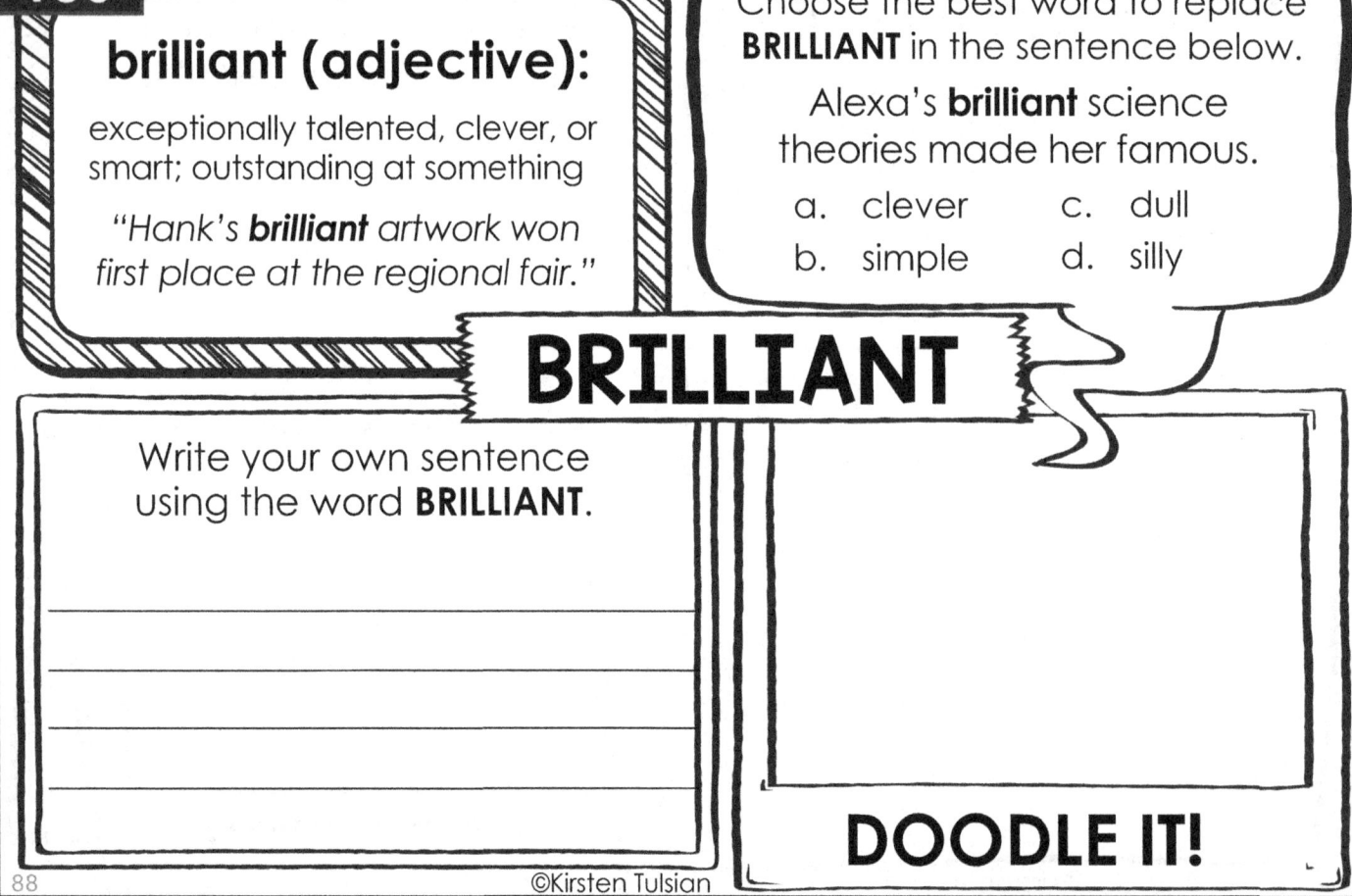

cope (verb):

to successfully deal with something difficult, like a problem or challenge

"I **cope** with stress by taking walks and writing in my journal."

Draw a picture of something you do to **cope** with challenges.

COPE

Write your own sentence using the word **COPE**.

Circle the **synonyms.**
- a. handle
- b. fail
- c. ignore
- d. survive
- e. manage
- f. give up

156

brilliant (adjective):

exceptionally talented, clever, or smart; outstanding at something

"Hank's **brilliant** artwork won first place at the regional fair."

Choose the best word to replace **BRILLIANT** in the sentence below.

Alexa's **brilliant** science theories made her famous.
- a. clever
- b. simple
- c. dull
- d. silly

BRILLIANT

Write your own sentence using the word **BRILLIANT**.

DOODLE IT!

157 delicate (adjective):

easily broken or damaged; fragile

*"The **delicate** flower lost its petals during the thunderstorm."*

Draw a picture of something **delicate**.

DELICATE

Write your own sentence using the word **DELICATE**.

Circle the **synonyms**.
a. fragile
b. strong
c. breakable
d. brittle
e. sturdy
f. tough

158 ponder (verb):

to think about something carefully and deeply, especially when trying to make a decision

*"When I play chess, I always **ponder** my next several moves before I decide on a strategy."*

Choose the best word(s) to replace **PONDERED** in the sentence below.

Nate gazed at the sunrise while he **pondered** his plans for the future.

a. forgot   c. evaluated
b. ignored   d. scoffed at

DOODLE IT!

PONDER

Write your own sentence using the word **PONDER**.

159

disturbance (noun):

something that disrupts; an interference or distraction

*"To avoid distractions and **disturbances**, I study in my bedroom with the door closed."*

Circle the **synonyms**.
a. commotion
b. confusion
c. peace
d. disruption
e. calm
f. interruption

DISTURBANCE

Write your own sentence using the word **DISTURBANCE**.

DOODLE IT!

160

erupt (verb):

to break or bust out suddenly; to burst out with something like laughter or anger

*"Scientists confirmed the volcano will **erupt** soon."*

Choose the best word to replace **ERUPTED** in the sentence below.

When she finished singing, the crowd **erupted** in applause.

a. exploded   c. whimpered
b. collapsed   d. whispered

ERUPT

Write your own sentence using the word **ERUPT**.

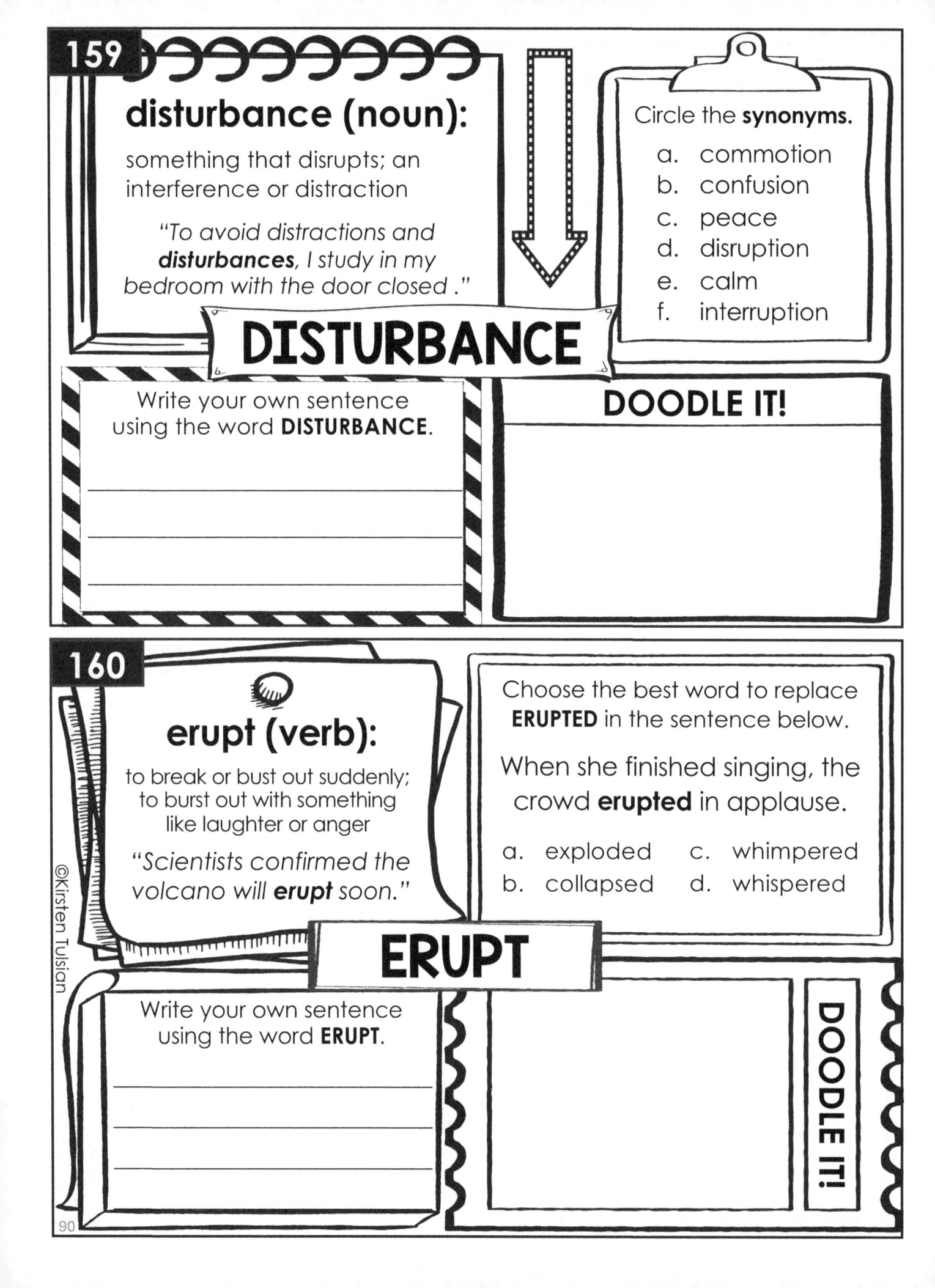

DOODLE IT!

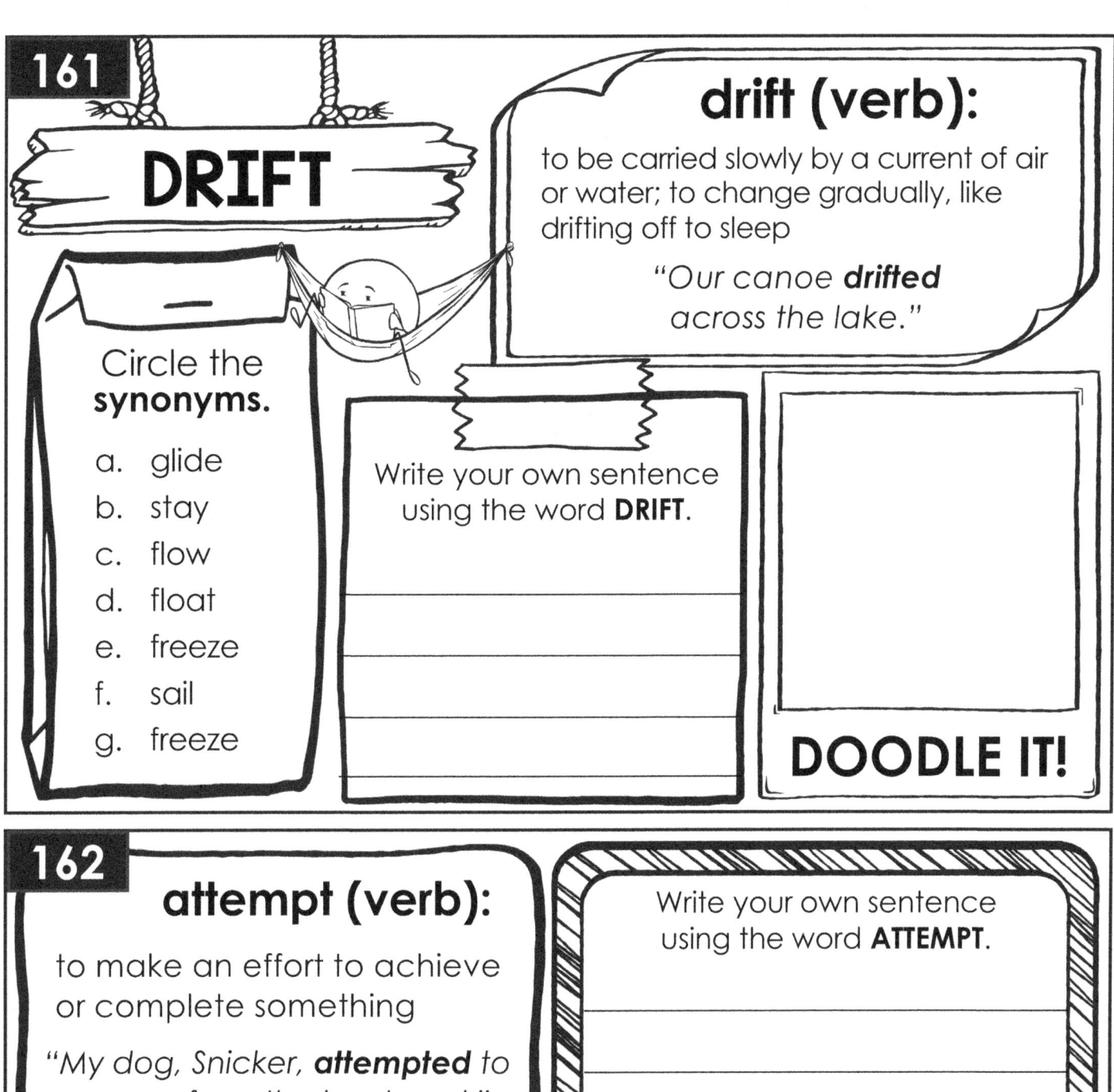

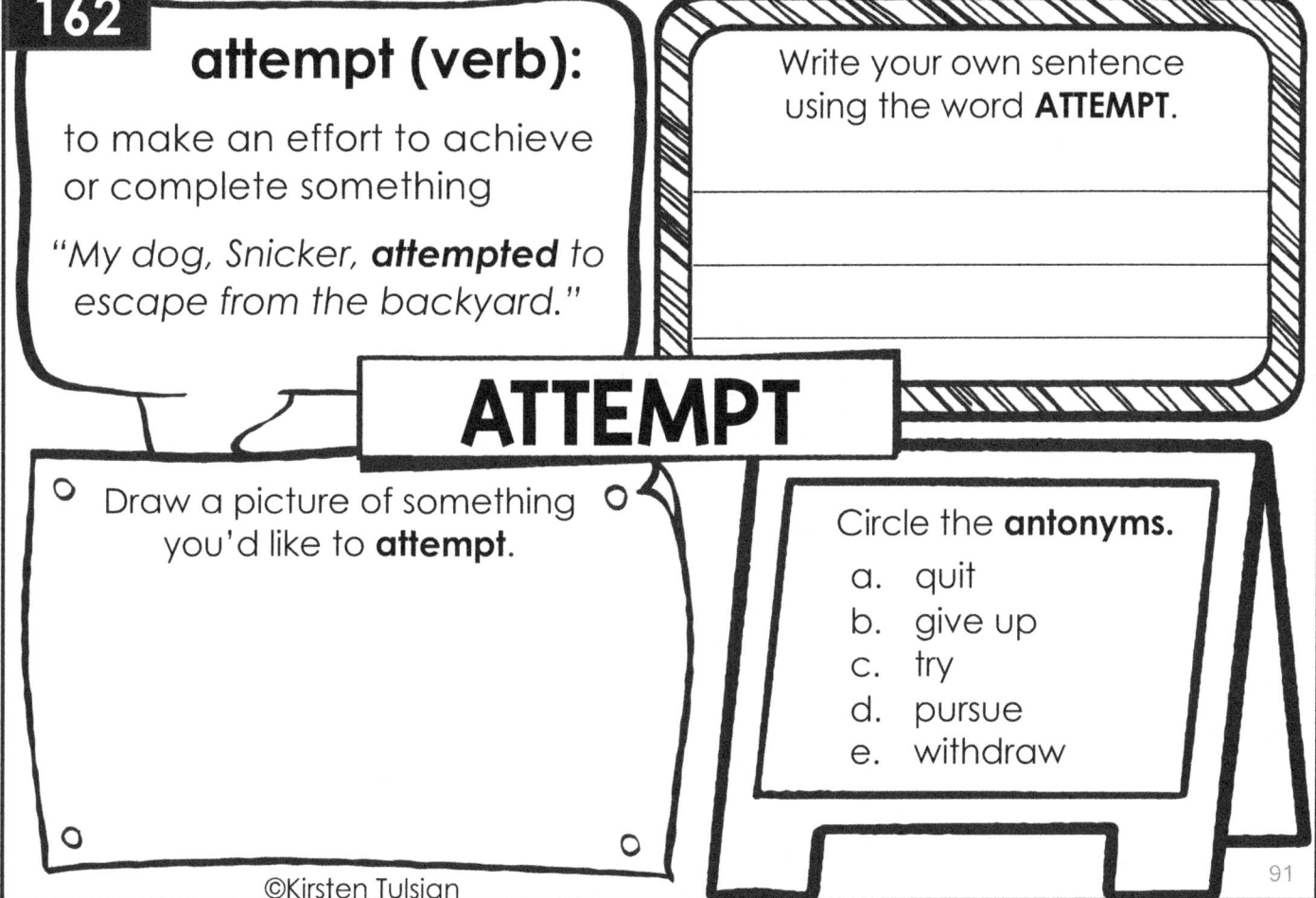

161 DRIFT

drift (verb): to be carried slowly by a current of air or water; to change gradually, like drifting off to sleep

"Our canoe **drifted** across the lake."

Circle the **synonyms**.
a. glide
b. stay
c. flow
d. float
e. freeze
f. sail
g. freeze

Write your own sentence using the word **DRIFT**.

DOODLE IT!

162 attempt (verb):

to make an effort to achieve or complete something

"My dog, Snicker, **attempted** to escape from the backyard."

Write your own sentence using the word **ATTEMPT**.

ATTEMPT

Draw a picture of something you'd like to **attempt**.

Circle the **antonyms**.
a. quit
b. give up
c. try
d. pursue
e. withdraw

163

miraculous (adjective):
super surprising and wonderful, like a miracle

"Sammy made a miraculous recovery once he got some much-needed rest."

Briefly describe a **miraculous** moment in your life.

MIRACULOUS

Write your own sentence using the word **MIRACULOUS**.

Circle the **synonyms.**
a. amazing
b. average
c. extraordinary
d. usual
e. marvelous
f. spectacular

164

ferocious (adjective):
fierce, violent, or wild, like a scary animal or strong storm

"The ferocious tiger snarled and growled, terrifying the kids at the zoo."

Choose the best word to replace **FEROCIOUS** in the sentence below.

The **ferocious** wind knocked down several trees in our neighborhood.
a. moderate   c. weak
b. intense   d. soft

FEROCIOUS

Circle the **synonyms.**
a. calm
b. fierce
c. ruthless
d. vicious
e. pleasant
f. gentle

Write your own sentence using the word **FEROCIOUS**.

DOODLE IT!

165

priority (noun):

the thing that is most important and must be done or dealt with first

*"Spending time with my family is always my **priority** on the weekends."*

DOODLE IT!

PRIORITY

Write your own sentence using the word **PRIORITY**.

Choose the best word to replace **PRIORITY** in the sentence below.

Feeding her pets is her first **priority** when she wakes up.

- a. delay
- b. oversight
- c. concern
- d. failure

166

agitate (verb):

to make someone feel nervous or upset; to stir something up

*"If you **agitate** a snake, it is more likely to bite."*

Choose the best word to replace **AGITATED** in the sentence below.

The loud noise **agitated** the baby, making her cry.

- a. settled
- b. quieted
- c. soothed
- d. disturbed

AGITATE

DOODLE IT!

Write your own sentence using the word **AGITATE**.

©Kirsten Tulsian

167

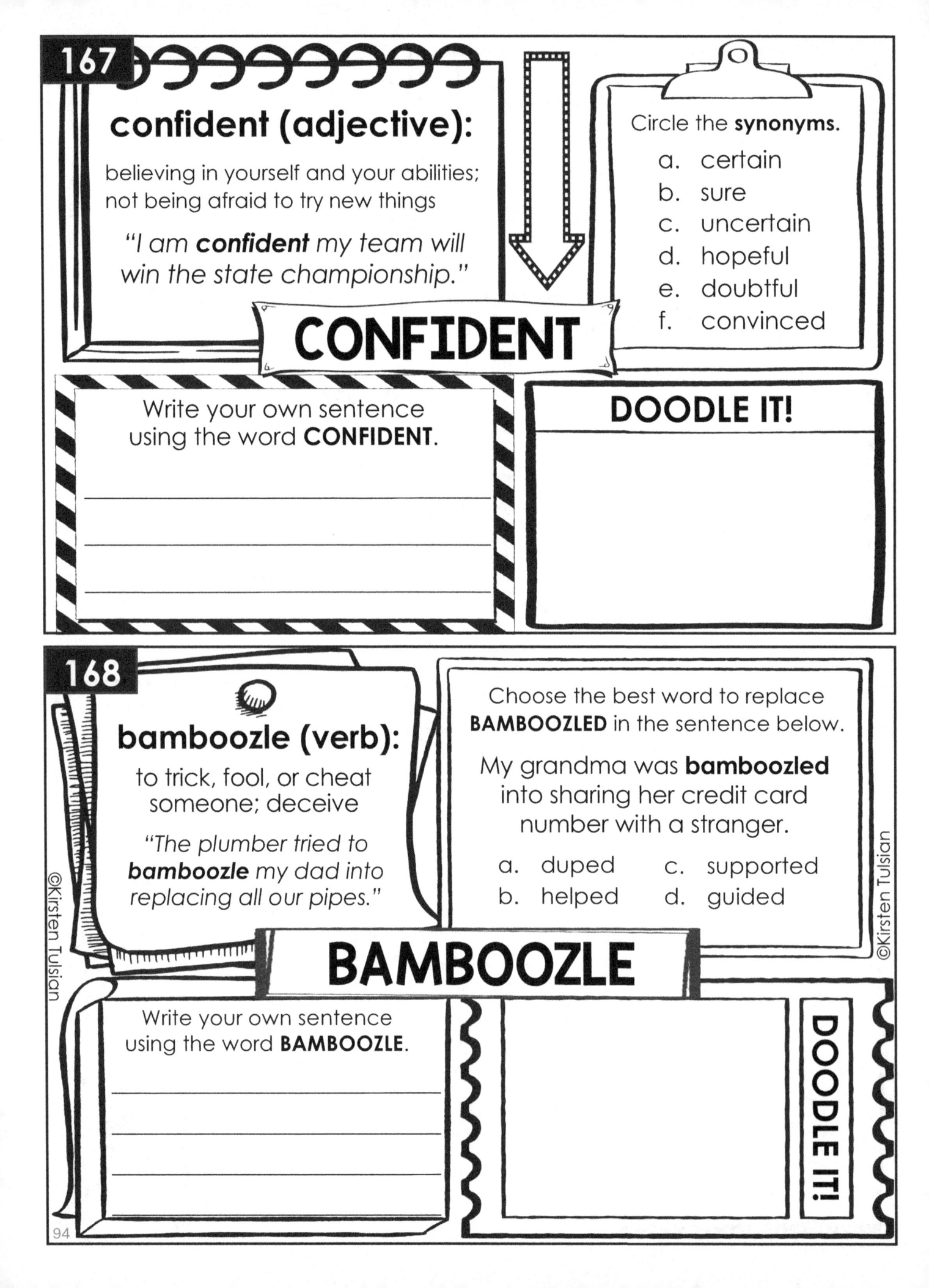

confident (adjective):

believing in yourself and your abilities; not being afraid to try new things

*"I am **confident** my team will win the state championship."*

CONFIDENT

Circle the **synonyms**.
a. certain
b. sure
c. uncertain
d. hopeful
e. doubtful
f. convinced

Write your own sentence using the word **CONFIDENT**.

DOODLE IT!

168

bamboozle (verb):

to trick, fool, or cheat someone; deceive

*"The plumber tried to **bamboozle** my dad into replacing all our pipes."*

Choose the best word to replace **BAMBOOZLED** in the sentence below.

My grandma was **bamboozled** into sharing her credit card number with a stranger.

a. duped   c. supported
b. helped   d. guided

BAMBOOZLE

Write your own sentence using the word **BAMBOOZLE**.

DOODLE IT!

169

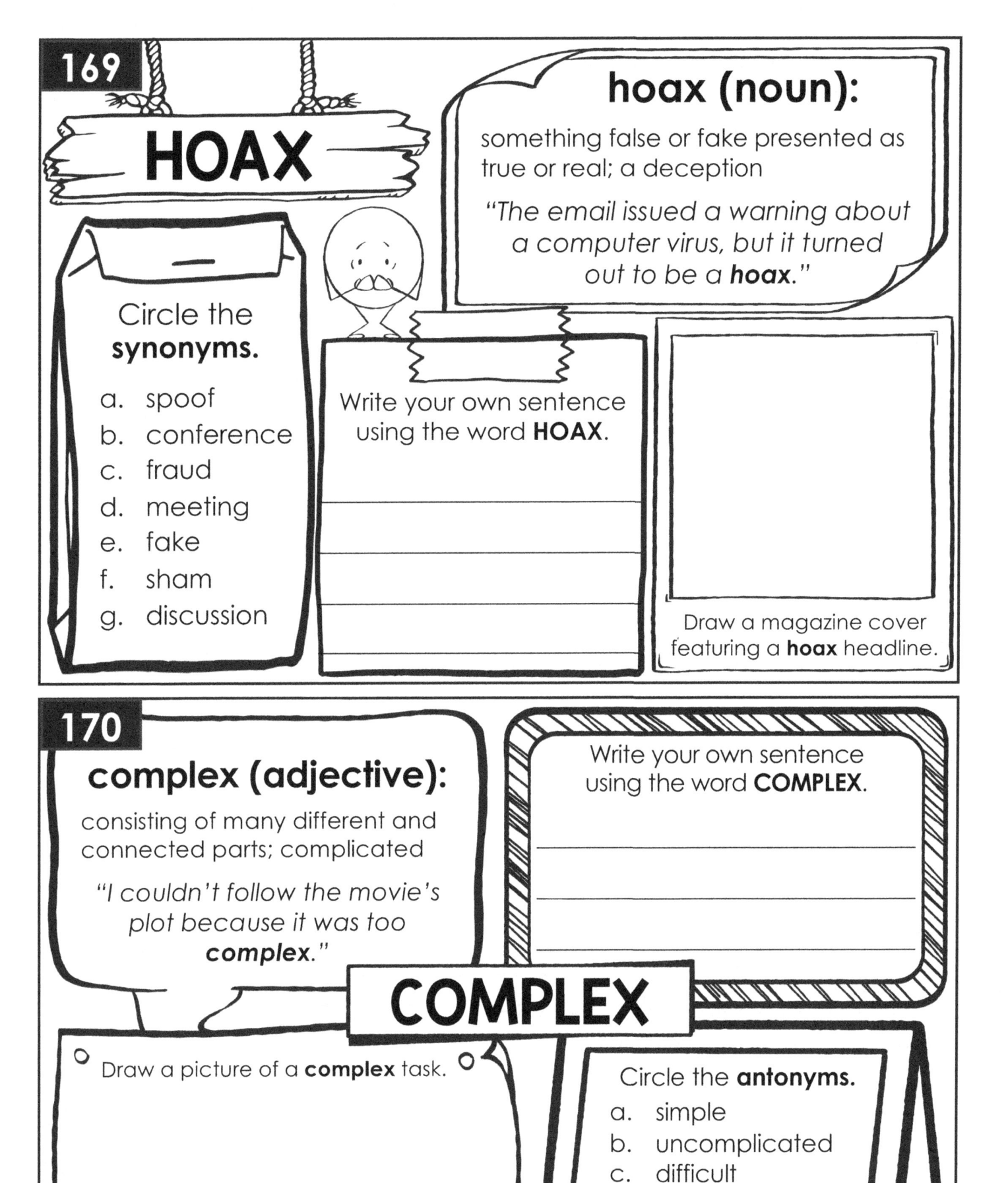

HOAX

hoax (noun): something false or fake presented as true or real; a deception

"The email issued a warning about a computer virus, but it turned out to be a hoax."

Circle the **synonyms.**

a. spoof
b. conference
c. fraud
d. meeting
e. fake
f. sham
g. discussion

Write your own sentence using the word **HOAX**.

Draw a magazine cover featuring a **hoax** headline.

170

complex (adjective): consisting of many different and connected parts; complicated

"I couldn't follow the movie's plot because it was too complex."

COMPLEX

Write your own sentence using the word **COMPLEX**.

Draw a picture of a **complex** task.

Circle the **antonyms.**

a. simple
b. uncomplicated
c. difficult
d. easy
e. complicated

171

scarce (adjective):

not easy to find or get; rare or in short supply

*"During the drought, fresh fruits and vegetables were **scarce**."*

How could a community work together if food became **scarce**?

_____
_____
_____
_____

SCARCE

Write your own sentence using the word **SCARCE**.

_____
_____
_____
_____

Circle the **synonyms**.
a. rare
b. sparse
c. plentiful
d. limited
e. ample
f. lacking

172

magnificent (adjective):

exceptionally good, beautiful, or impressive

*"We have a **magnificent** view of downtown from our hotel room."*

Choose the best word to replace **MAGNIFICENT** in the sentence below.

Meditating by the waterfall was a **magnificent** experience.

a. mundane   c. typical
b. glorious   d. ordinary

MAGNIFICENT

Circle the **antonyms**.
a. unimpressive
b. common
c. majestic
d. average
e. regular
f. impressive

Write your own sentence using the word **MAGNIFICENT**.

_____
_____
_____
_____

DOODLE IT!

©Kirsten Tulsian

173 pending (adjective):

awaiting a decision or settlement; not yet decided

*"Customers have been asking about **pending** price increases on groceries."*

PENDING

How do you like to pass the time when you're waiting on something?

Write your own sentence using the word **PENDING**.

Circle the **synonyms**.
a. unsettled
b. unresolved
c. confirmed
d. undecided
e. decided
f. resolved

174 atypical (adjective):

not normal or typical; unusual or different from what is expected

*"Eating meat would be very **atypical** behavior for a vegan or vegetarian."*

DOODLE IT!

ATYPICAL

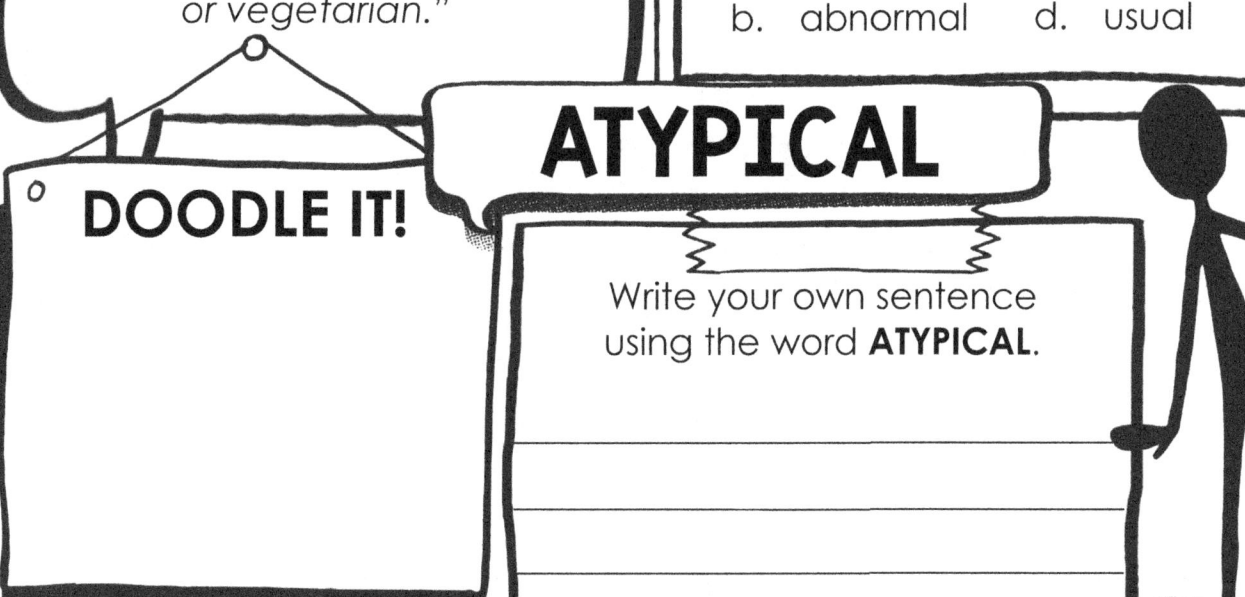

Choose the best word to replace **ATYPICAL** in the sentence below.

We're going to the vet because my snake is displaying **atypical** behavior.

a. common
b. abnormal
c. ordinary
d. usual

Write your own sentence using the word **ATYPICAL**.

175

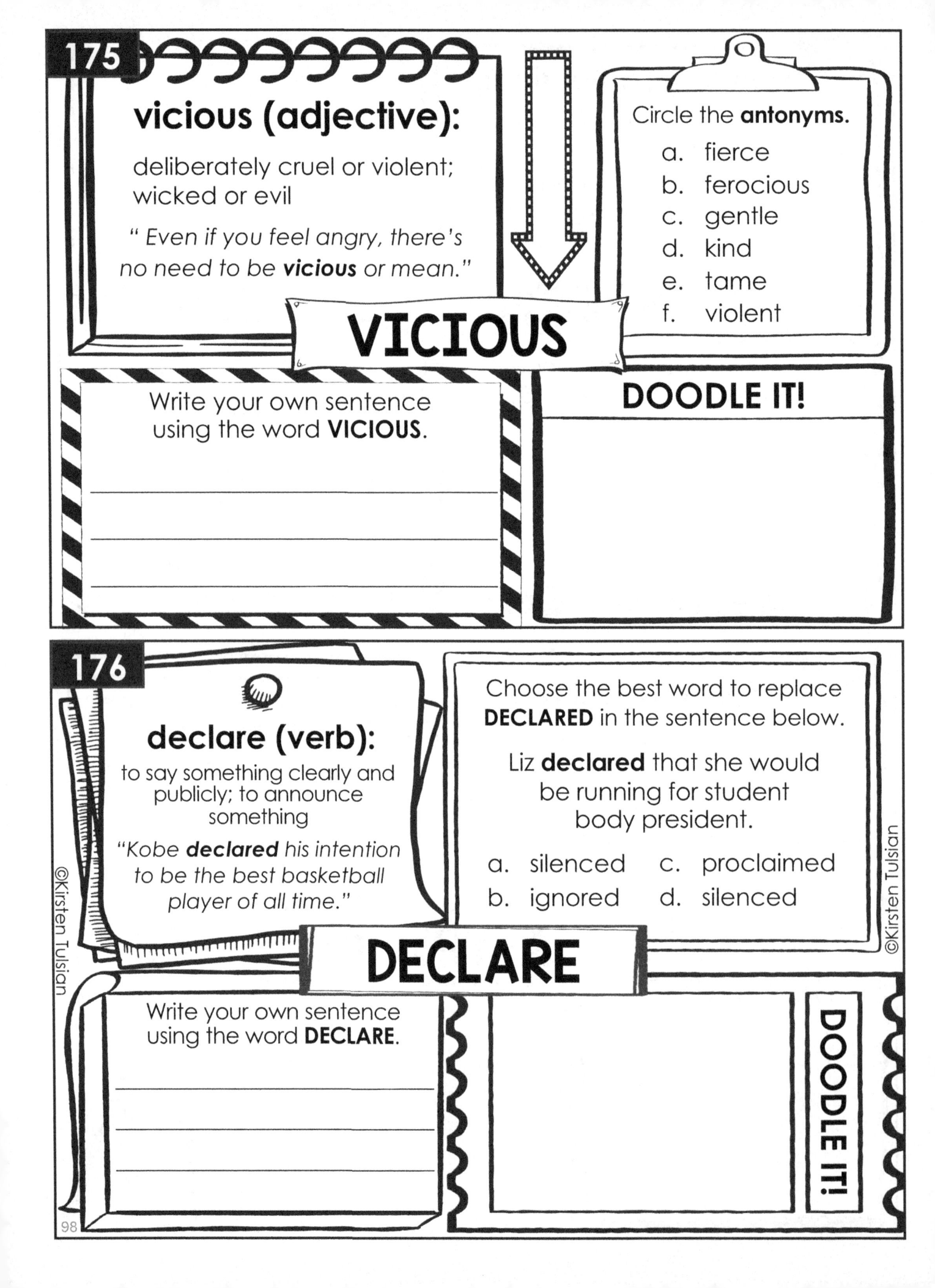

vicious (adjective):

deliberately cruel or violent; wicked or evil

"Even if you feel angry, there's no need to be **vicious** or mean."

VICIOUS

Circle the **antonyms**.
a. fierce
b. ferocious
c. gentle
d. kind
e. tame
f. violent

Write your own sentence using the word **VICIOUS**.

DOODLE IT!

176

declare (verb):

to say something clearly and publicly; to announce something

"Kobe **declared** his intention to be the best basketball player of all time."

DECLARE

Choose the best word to replace **DECLARED** in the sentence below.

Liz **declared** that she would be running for student body president.

a. silenced   c. proclaimed
b. ignored   d. silenced

Write your own sentence using the word **DECLARE**.

DOODLE IT!

177

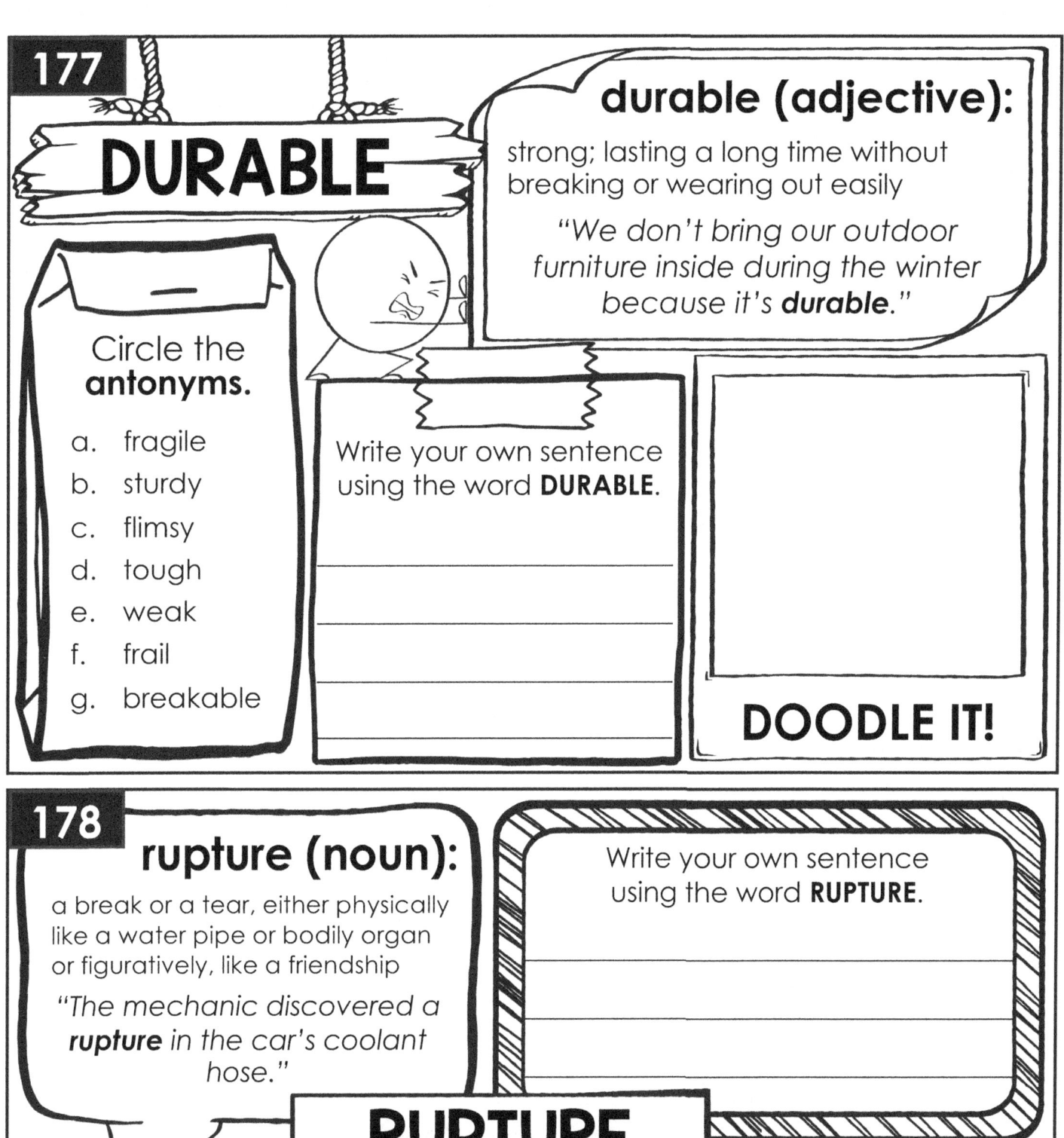

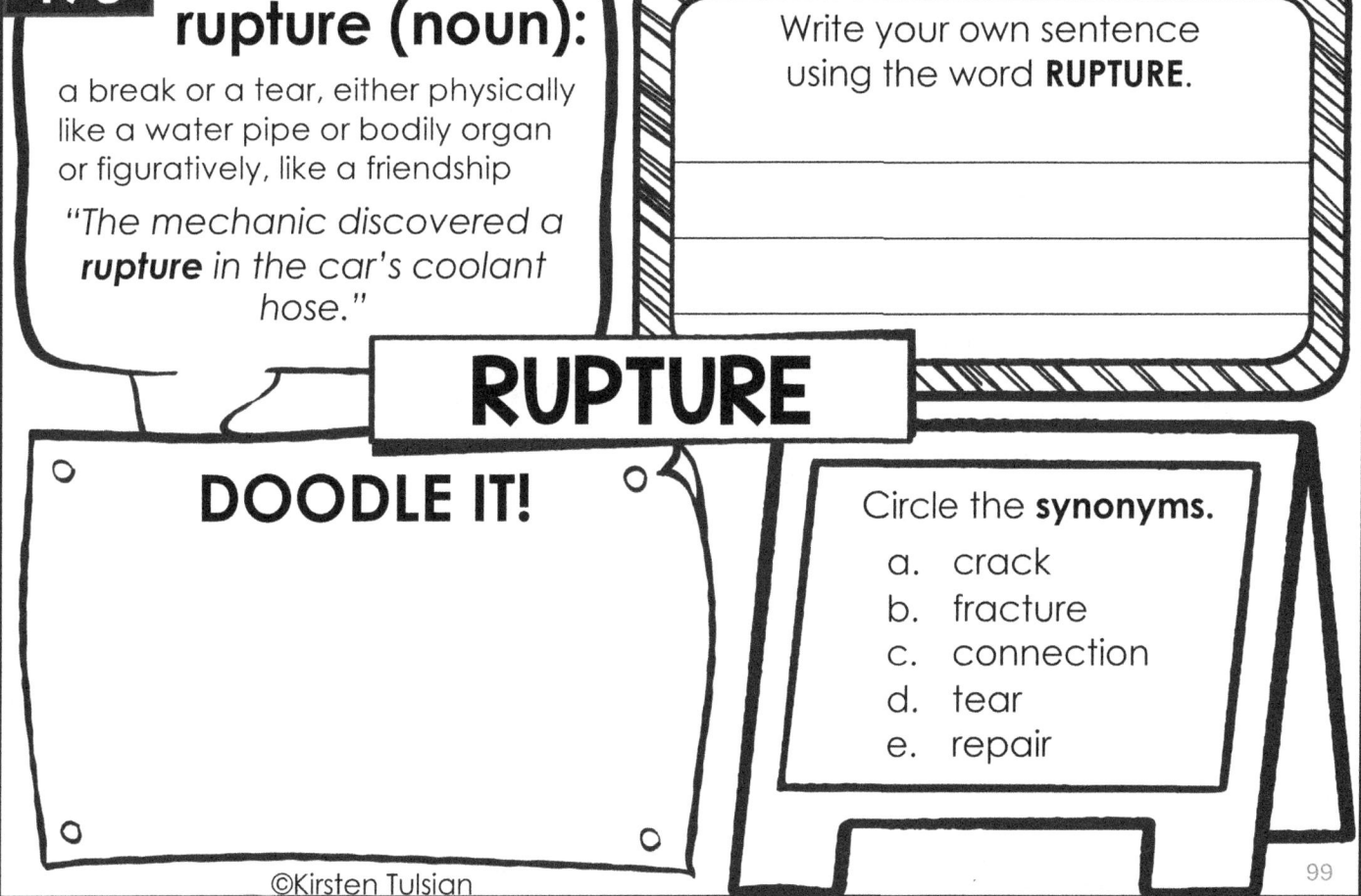

DURABLE

durable (adjective): strong; lasting a long time without breaking or wearing out easily

*"We don't bring our outdoor furniture inside during the winter because it's **durable**."*

Circle the **antonyms**.
a. fragile
b. sturdy
c. flimsy
d. tough
e. weak
f. frail
g. breakable

Write your own sentence using the word **DURABLE**.

DOODLE IT!

178

rupture (noun): a break or a tear, either physically like a water pipe or bodily organ or figuratively, like a friendship

*"The mechanic discovered a **rupture** in the car's coolant hose."*

Write your own sentence using the word **RUPTURE**.

RUPTURE

DOODLE IT!

Circle the **synonyms**.
a. crack
b. fracture
c. connection
d. tear
e. repair

179

equivalent (adjective):

equal in value, force, measure, or meaning

"One foot is **equivalent** to 12 inches."

DOODLE IT!

EQUIVALENT

Write your own sentence using the word **EQUIVALENT**.

Circle the **synonyms**.
a. similar
b. same
c. equal
d. different
e. identical
f. unequal

180

shenanigans (noun):

a funny, mischievous, or silly prank or action

"Spot and Muffin escaped and got into some **shenanigans** with the neighbor's dog."

Choose the best word to replace SHENANIGANS in the sentence below.

Ginger was up to her usual **shenanigans** today.

a. mischief   c. goodness
b. seriousness   d. kindness

SHENANIGANS

Circle the **synonyms**.
a. mischief
b. seriousness
c. horseplay
d. nonsense
e. obedience

Write your own sentence using the word **SHENANIGANS**.

©Kirsten Tulsian

ANSWER KEY

Where correct answers apply, find them on the following pages.

*Accept any reasonable response in sections where students draw a picture or write a sentence.

ANSWER KEY: Where correct answers apply, find them here. *Accept any reasonable response in sections where students draw a picture or write a sentence.*

1. QUEASY synonyms: a, e, f, h	2. SIGNIFICANT antonyms: a, b, e	3. WITHDRAW synonyms: a, b, d	4. WISDOM word replacement: a antonyms: c, d
5. MOTIVE word replacement: a	6. OUTSTANDING word replacement: c	7. ABSURD synonyms: a, b, f	8. TURBULENT word replacement: d
9. STINT synonyms: a, d, f, g	10. ACHIEVEMENT antonyms: a, d	11. BENEFICIAL synonyms: a, b, d	12. PROFOUND word replacement: b antonyms: c, d, f
13. TRANQUIL synonyms: a, b, d, f	14. AMBITIOUS word replacement: c	15. EMBARK synonyms: a, d, e	16. ENCOUNTER word replacement: d
17. AVID antonyms: a, d, f, g	18. SCAVENGER synonyms: a, c, d	19. TRIVIAL synonyms: a, d, f	20. BOISTEROUS word replacement: d antonyms: b, c, e
21. MASSIVE word replacement: b	22. GROTESQUE word replacement: b	23. CONVINCE synonyms: b, c, e	24. CONTINUOUS word replacement: c
25. DECAY synonyms: b, c, f	26. ACKNOWLEDGE antonyms: a, b, e	27. FLUSTERED synonyms: b, c, d	28. ASTOUND word replacement: b
29. VENTURE word replacement: b	30. REJUVENATE word replacement: b	31. INVESTIGATE synonyms: a, b, f	32. MAINTAIN word replacement: c
33. ALOOF synonyms: a, c, d, e	34. PRECISION antonyms: b, d	35. REMORSE synonyms: a, c, d, f	36. PREDICT word replacement: b
37. BIZARRE synonyms: b, c, e	38. DISCREET word replacement: d	39. ANGUISH synonyms: b, c, d, f	40. NURTURE word replacement: c

ANSWER KEY: Where correct answers apply, find them here. *Accept any reasonable response in sections where students draw a picture or write a sentence.*

41. BLAND synonyms: a, d, e	42. OBNOXIOUS antonyms: a, b, d	43. RIGOROUS synonyms: b, d, e	44. DISGRUNTLED word replacement: a antonyms: a, b, e
45. EFFICIENT word replacement: c	46. PEDESTRIAN word replacement: b	47. DEVOUR synonyms: a, c, e	48. DEBRIS word replacement: b
49. EPIC synonyms: a, c, d, g	50. EXQUISITE antonym: c, d	51. POTENTIAL synonyms: c, d, f	52. AWKWARD word replacement: c antonyms: a, b, d
53. IMMENSE synonyms: a, c, f	54. BECKON word replacement: a	55. SUITABLE synonyms: a, c, d	56. PECULIAR word replacement: b
57. ABRUPT antonyms: b, d, g	58. EXAMINE synonyms: a, d, e	59. BANTER synonyms: b, d, e	60. SUBTLE word replacement: a synonyms: b, e
61. DUPLICATE word replacement: b	62. UNBELIEVABLE word replacement: d	63. DISTRAUGHT synonyms: b, c, d	64. STURDY word replacement: a
65. DETECT synonyms: c, d, f, g	66. VIBRANT antonyms: b, d, e	67. TRIUMPH synonyms: a, c, d, e	68. FASCINATE word replacement: b
69. NAVIGATE word replacement: b	70. ORDEAL word replacement: c	71. PERCEPTIVE synonyms: b, c, d, f	72. MEANDER word replacement: d
73. RECITE synonyms: a, d, e, g	74. OBVIOUS antonyms: b, d, e	75. EXCLUDE synonyms: b, c, e	76. MURKY word replacement: b
77. ENHANCE synonyms: a, b, d	78. SCOFF word replacement: a	79. PERPLEXED synonyms: a, b, e, f	80. HAZARDOUS word replacement: c

©Kirsten Tulsian

ANSWER KEY: Where correct answers apply, find them here. *Accept any reasonable response in sections where students draw a picture or write a sentence.*

81. LURK synonyms: a, b, d, f	82. NOTEWORTHY antonyms: a, c, d	83. VIVID synonyms: a, b, d, f	84. BEWILDER word replacement: c synonyms: a, c, d
85. AGILE word replacement: d	86. SOLITARY word replacement: c	87. RETRIEVE synonyms: a, c, e	88. RUBBLE word replacement: c
89. LURE synonyms: a, d, e, g	90. VISIBLE antonyms: a, c, d	91. PROVOKE synonyms: b, d, f	92. DISCARD word replacement: d antonyms: b, d, f
93. RELUCTANT synonyms: a, b, d	94. MINIATURE word replacement: b	95. IDENTICAL antonyms: b, c, e	96. ILLUMINATE word replacement: d
97. IRATE antonyms: b, e, g	98. WANDER synonyms: b, c, e	99. ESSENTIAL synonyms: a, b, c, e	100. DESTRUCTIVE word replacement: d synonyms: b, c, e
101. EXAGGERATE word replacement: b	102. BENEFIT word replacement: d	103. SWELTER synonyms: b, c, e	104. DOLLOP word replacement: b
105. TIDY synonyms: a, b, d, e, f	106. EFFECTIVE antonyms: a, b, d	107. FABULOUS synonyms: a, c, d, e	108. TRANSFORM word replacement: b
109. TRAGIC word replacement: c	110. ENABLE word replacement: a	111. JAGGED synonyms: a, c, d	112. FORTUNATE word replacement: c
113. EXPAND synonyms: a, b, d, f	114. INDULGE antonyms: b, c, e	115. ENVY synonyms: a, d, e	116. TENDER word replacement: a
117. HAZY synonyms: b, c, e, f	118. LINGER word replacement: d	119. BLUNDER synonyms: b, c, d	120. PERISH word replacement: b

©Kirsten Tulsian

ANSWER KEY: Where correct answers apply, find them here. *Accept any reasonable response in sections where students draw a picture or write a sentence.*

121. PLEAD synonyms: b, c, e, g	122. AVOID antonyms: c, d, e	123. HOSTILE synonyms: b, c, e	124. FIASCO word replacement: c synonyms: a, c, e
125. ARID word replacement: d	126. WRANGLE word replacement: c	127. FRANTIC synonyms: a, c, d, f	128. LETHARGIC word replacement: c
129. SWARM synonyms: a, b, d, f	130. ACQUIRE antonyms: a, c, e	131. ABANDON synonyms: a, c, e, f	132. ANXIOUS word replacement: b antonyms: a, b, d
133. EMPATHY synonyms: a, c, d	134. FEEBLE word replacement: a	135. STRIVE antonyms: a, c, d	136. NOTIFY word replacement: b
137. UNRULY antonyms: a, c, e, g	138. PREVENT synonyms: a, b, e	139. SENSITIVE synonyms: b, c, e	140. MIMIC word replacement: d synonyms: a, c, d
141. RECYCLE word replacement: d	142. PURSUE word replacement: d	143. PLENTIFUL synonyms: a, b, d	144. PROSPER word replacement: d
145. HAVEN synonyms: a, d, e, g	146. BURDEN antonyms: a, b, d	147. DAZZLE synonyms: a, c, d, e	148. CLARIFY word replacement: c
149. CONTRIBUTE word replacement: b	150. DOZE word replacement: d	151. UNIQUE synonyms: a, c, e	152. ARROGANT word replacement: c
153. VAST synonyms: a, b, d, e	154. CONSULT antonyms: b, c, e	155. COPE synonyms: a, d, e	156. BRILLIANT word replacement: a
157. DELICATE synonyms: a, c, d	158. PONDER word replacement: c	159. DISTURBANCE synonyms: a, b, d, f	160. ERUPT word replacement: a

©Kirsten Tulsian

ANSWER KEY: Where correct answers apply, find them here. **Accept any reasonable response in sections where students draw a picture or write a sentence.**

161. DRIFT synonyms: a, c, d, f	162. ATTEMPT antonyms: a, b, e	163. MIRACULOUS synonyms: a, c, e, f	164. FEROCIOUS word preplacement: b synonyms: b, c, d
165. PRIORITY word replacement: c	166. AGITATE word replacement: d	167. CONFIDENT synonyms: a, b, d, f	168. BAMBOOZLE word replacement: a
169. HOAX synonyms: a, c, e, f	170. COMPLEX antonyms: a, b, d	171. SCARCE synonyms: a, b, d, f	172. MAGNIFICENT word replacement: b antonyms: a, b, d, e
173. PENDING synonyms: a, b, d	174. ATYPICAL word replacement: b	175. VICIOUS antonyms: c, d, e	176. DECLARE word replacement: c
177. DURABLE antonyms: a, c, e, f, g	178. RUPTURE synonyms: a, b, d	179. EQUIVALENT synonyms: a, b, c, e	180. SHENANIGANS word replacement: a synonyms: a, c, d

©Kirsten Tulsian

About the Author:

Kirsten Tulsian is a former elementary teacher and school counselor of 18 years. She has a Bachelor's Degree in Psychology and Elementary Education from the University of Iowa and a Master's Degree in School Counseling from Sam Houston State University. As the owner of Kirsten's Kaboodle, she is passionate about nurturing kids in heart and mind. She currently resides in Salt Lake City, where she creates social-emotional learning and language arts activities and resources for parents and educators. You can find her at kirstenskaboodle.com.

Join her email list for free PDF resources, tips, updates, and important information:
kirstenskaboodle.com/subscribe

Interested in additional workbooks created by this author?

Scan the QR code below:

Made in the USA
Columbia, SC
26 October 2025